Powerhouse

An Intermediate Business English Course

D1370554

David Evans
with Grammar Reference
by Peter Strutt

CONTENTS 3

1 connections

General business VOCABULARY

TELL ME, WHAT ARE YOU?

In the Hollywood movie *Big Night*, one of the characters gives a definition of a businessperson.

Work with a partner. Discuss the definition below. Do you agree with him? Why – or why not? Compare your ideas with others in the class.

'I'm a businessman. I am anything I need to be at any time. Tell me, what exactly are you?'

YOU AND YOUR JOB Work with a partner. Which of these is the main focus of your work? Explain why.

your product	customers	money	other people

YOU AND YOUR WORK Work with a partner. Which of these best describes the kind of organisation that you work for? Give a few details.

a multinational	I don't work for an organisation.	a government body
a medium-sized company	a small business	an institution

AN AVERAGE WORKER? In this text, two American management writers try to define an 'average worker'. Quickly scan the text and find the words which match these definitions:

1 an organisation that represents workers
2 a husband or wife
3 the age at which people normally stop working.

 Work with a partner. Check your answers.

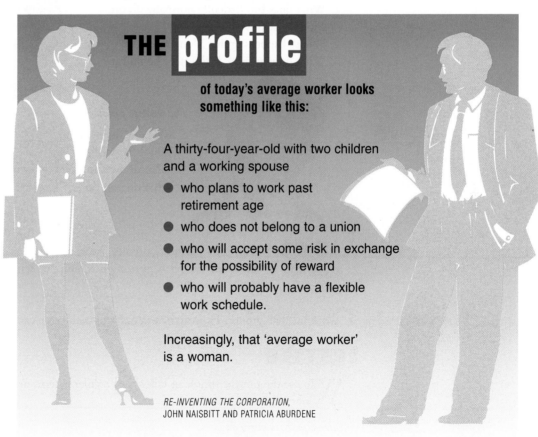

THE **profile**

of today's average worker looks something like this:

A thirty-four-year-old with two children and a working spouse

● who plans to work past retirement age

● who does not belong to a union

● who will accept some risk in exchange for the possibility of reward

● who will probably have a flexible work schedule.

Increasingly, that 'average worker' is a woman.

RE-INVENTING THE CORPORATION,
JOHN NAISBITT AND PATRICIA ABURDENE

THE AVERAGE WORKER AND YOU

1 Work with a partner. Read the text carefully. Explain to your partner in what ways you are similar to the average worker. In what ways are you different?

2 Go round the class and take turns to explain what you have learnt about the other members of the class. (Don't talk about yourself!)

G R A M M A R   R E V I E W

NORMALLY OR NOW?

1 Match the four questions on the left with four appropriate answers on the right.

1 What do you do?
2 What are you doing in this class?
3 Where do you live?
4 Where are you staying?

a In a hotel in the centre of town.
b I work for a large company.
c I'm learning English.
d I've got a house in New York.

2 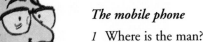 Work with a partner. Look at the forms of the questions and explain why different tenses are used.

TWO BUSINESS FAILURES

1  Work with a partner. Listen and then answer the questions below.

The office

1 What does Bill Radcliffe normally do on Monday at this time?
2 What's happening this Monday?
3 What do you think is the story behind it?

The mobile phone

1 Where is the man?
2 Why is he calling Clara?
3 What do he and Clara do every month?
4 What do you think Clara says at the end of the call?

2 Work with a partner. Listen to the scenes again and notice the use of two tenses – one tense to talk about what is happening now and one tense to talk about what normally happens.

3 Work in small groups. How many examples of each tense can you remember from the tape?

CHECK

We use the present simple to talk about regular actions or normal situations.

I drive to work every day.

We use the present continuous to talk about a temporary situation or something that's happening now.

I'm driving a hired car this week.
I'm looking out of the window.

▌ *For more on these tenses, turn to page 141* ▌

The present

SCULLEY AND JOBS

John Sculley

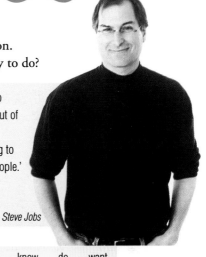

Steve Jobs

Here is a conversation between John Sculley (at that time a top executive for Pepsi Cola) and Steve Jobs (at that time head of Apple Computers).

1 Work with a partner. Read the conversation. What do you think Steve Jobs wants John Sculley to do?

'Steve, why are you talking to me?' I asked. 'Why don't you go talk to somebody at IBM or Hewlett Packard? Why do you want someone out of the soft drink industry. I don't know anything about computers.'
'What we're doing has never been done before,' he said. 'We're trying to build a totally different kind of company and we need really great people.'

This extract comes from Odyssey, *John Sculley's story of his life at Pepsi and Apple.*

2 Underline these verbs in the text.

| need | try | know | do | want |

Work with a partner. Are these verbs talking about things which normally happen or things which are happening now? Why do you think those forms of the verbs are used?

CHECK

There are some verbs which are almost never used in the present continuous. Most of them come in these four categories:

1 Verbs of the mind, e.g. *think, know, understand*
2 Verbs of feeling, e.g. *like, love, hate*
3 Verbs of the senses, e.g. *see, hear, taste*
4 Verbs of wanting and possession, e.g. *want, need, own.*

❚ *For more on this, turn to page 141* ❚

PRACTICE

1 Work with a partner.

A: Look out of the window and answer B's questions.
B: Ask questions about what is happening outside.
(What's happening outside?
A man's getting out of his car.
Where's he going?
Into a shop.)

2 Work with a partner. Ask and answer questions on these subjects:

❚ your daily work routine (e.g. When do you arrive at work in the morning?)
❚ your main interests (e.g. What do you do at the weekend?)
❚ your holidays (e.g. Where do you usually go?).

doing **business** *Answering the phone*

AHOY!   After the invention of the telephone in 1876, there was one immediate problem: what do you say when you answer it?

1 What four ways of answering the telephone are described here?

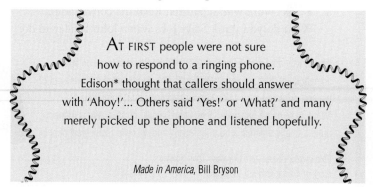

> AT FIRST people were not sure how to respond to a ringing phone. Edison* thought that callers should answer with 'Ahoy!'... Others said 'Yes!' or 'What?' and many merely picked up the phone and listened hopefully.
>
> *Made in America*, Bill Bryson

▌ GLOSSARY ▌

* Thomas Edison *an American inventor*

2 How do you answer the phone in English ...

▌ when you're at work?   ▌ when you're in a hotel room?
▌ when you're at home?   ▌ when your mobile phone rings?

Compare what you say with others.

GLENGARRY GLEN ROSS   The film *Glengarry Glen Ross* starts with a businessman called Sheldon Levene making a phone call. We don't hear what the person on the other end of the line says, but you can probably guess.

1 Can you put the sentences below into the correct places in the dialogue?

1 Just a moment, please.
2 Can he call you back?
3 No, it's me again.
4 No, I'm afraid he's in a meeting.
5 No, I'm sorry he's not here.
6 Hello. Dr Lowenstein's office.
7 Is it urgent?
8 Could you tell me your name, please?
9 Hello.

RECEPTIONIST	a _____
LEVENE	Could I speak to Dr Lowenstein, please?
RECEPTIONIST	b _____
LEVENE	Well, it's rather important. Could you get him for me?
RECEPTIONIST	c _____
	(PAUSE)
RECEPTIONIST	d _____
LEVENE	Ah, doctor ...
RECEPTIONIST	e _____
LEVENE	Well, could you get ...?
RECEPTIONIST	f _____
LEVENE	What do you mean? He's not there? I have to speak to him.
RECEPTIONIST	g _____
LEVENE	Yes, it is fairly urgent.
RECEPTIONIST	h _____
LEVENE	Mr Levene.
RECEPTIONIST	i _____
LEVENE	No, I can't be reached. I'll get back to him.

2 Look again at the film script and underline the phrases that Sheldon Levene uses ...

1 ... to ask to speak to Dr Lowenstein.

2 ... to say he'll phone again later.

PHONE PHRASES

1 In this table, make a summary of some telephoning phrases from the dialogue above. Compare your answers.

Asking to speak to someone	
What you hear if the person is not available	
Asking someone to wait	
Asking for the other person's name	
Saying that you'll phone again later	

2  Think of at least one other phrase for each of the five functions above.

PHONE ROLES

Take turns to play the roles of caller and receptionist in these situations.

1 RECEPTIONIST   Answer phone   Say that he's in a meeting

     CALLER   Ask to speak to Carlos   Say you'll phone later

2 RECEPTIONIST   Answer phone   Ask caller to wait — Ask caller's name

     CALLER   Ask to speak to Carlos   Give name

3 The caller urgently wants to speak to Carlos, but the receptionist knows that Carlos is busy and doesn't want to speak on the phone.

Glengarry Glen Ross is a film about salesmen working in an American real estate office. It was written by the top American playwright, David Mamet.

doing **business** *Getting through*

THE RIGHT PERSON

Less than 30% of business calls get through to the right person at the first attempt. How difficult is it to get through to you at work?

1 Which of these do you have?

a secretary answerphone

voice mail *a receptionist*

2 Do you have other ways of <u>not</u> answering the phone yourself? Compare your answers in small groups.

PHONE VERBS

Phone conversations use a lot of phrasal verbs (verb + preposition).

1 Match the phrasal verbs in the column on the left to the phrases with similar meanings in the column on the right.

1	to get through	*a*	to connect
2	to put through	*b*	to be connected
3	to cut off	*c*	to disconnect
4	to hang up	*d*	to wait
5	to hold on	*e*	to put down the receiver

2  What other phrasal verbs do you know that are often used on the phone?

NOT GETTING THROUGH!

1 📼 Listen to the five telephone conversations. As you listen, make a note of the problems that George Coy faces in the box on the opposite page. (There is sometimes more than one problem per call.)

2 Compare your answers.

3 What questions do the speakers use to solve some of the problems? Write the questions next to the relevant problems.

	PROBLEM	QUESTION
Conversation 1		
Conversation 2		
Conversation 3		
Conversation 4		
Conversation 5		

4 Check your answers by listening again.

PHONE ROLES Take turns to be the caller and the receptionist in these situations. Make sure that you finish each conversation in a satisfactory way.

▌ The caller wants to speak to Jane Williamson, but her line is busy.
▌ The caller wants to speak to George Aaranow, who, unfortunately, has left the company.
▌ The caller wants to speak to Dave Moss but it's difficult to hear because there is a lot of interference on the line.
▌ The caller wants to speak to Mrs Baylen, but gets a wrong number.

focus

Culture and communication

A TALE OF TWO CULTURES

Colonel Younghusband

The text below is about two very different cultures, British and Tibetan.

1 Read the story and answer these questions.

1 What did the Tibetans think they were communicating?

2 What did the British think the Tibetans were communicating?

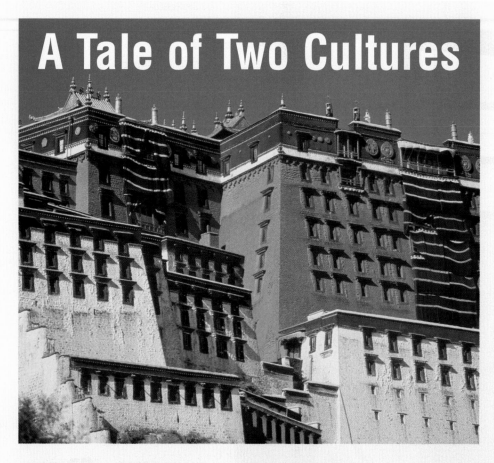

A Tale of Two Cultures

WHEN British soldiers entered the Forbidden City of Lhasa, Tibet, in the summer of 1904, their leader, Colonel Francis Younghusband, saw crowds of local people clapping and cheering. Colonel Younghusband thought it was a friendly welcome – but he was very wrong.

A Tibetan writer explained the other point of view:

'When the British officers marched to the Tsuglakhang and other places, the inhabitants of Lhasa were displeased. They shouted and chanted to bring down rain, and made clapping gestures to repulse them. In the foreigner's custom, these are seen as signs of welcome, so they took off their hats and said thank you.'

2 Do you know any similar stories? In groups, think of examples of common expressions or gestures in one culture which people from another culture might not understand.

A CULTURE QUESTIONNAIRE

Fons Trompenaars is a Dutch expert on business and culture. He interviewed over 15,000 business people in fifty countries to find out how culture affects business life. Here are a few of the questions that he asked.

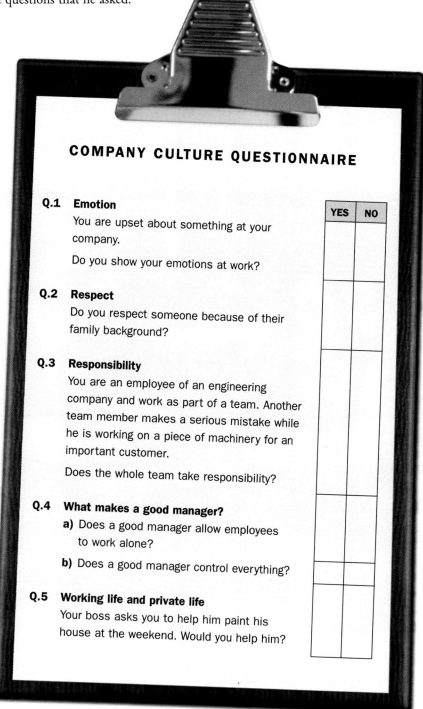

COMPANY CULTURE QUESTIONNAIRE

		YES	NO
Q.1	**Emotion** You are upset about something at your company. Do you show your emotions at work?		
Q.2	**Respect** Do you respect someone because of their family background?		
Q.3	**Responsibility** You are an employee of an engineering company and work as part of a team. Another team member makes a serious mistake while he is working on a piece of machinery for an important customer. Does the whole team take responsibility?		
Q.4	**What makes a good manager?** a) Does a good manager allow employees to work alone? b) Does a good manager control everything?		
Q.5	**Working life and private life** Your boss asks you to help him paint his house at the weekend. Would you help him?		

1 Work in small groups and discuss your answers, giving examples, when relevant.

2 Now turn to page 124 and compare your answers to the results of surveys of managers in several different countries. In your groups, discuss:

1 Do any of the results surprise you?
2 Can you see any general trends? What are they?
3 What does this tell you about doing business in different cultures?

Introductions

social skills

**INTRODUCING
YOURSELF ...**

In this scene from the film *Glengarry Glen Ross*, an American salesman is talking to a customer in a bar.

1 Look at the script and underline the following:

1 the phrase that Roma uses to give his name
2 the phrase he uses to ask for the other person's name
3 the formal phrase he uses to greet the other person.

Here, the real estate salesman Richard Roma is trying to sell a new house to James Lingk.

ROMA Hmmm ... It's been a long day. What are you drinking?

LINGK Gimlet.

ROMA Well, let's have a couple more. My name is Richard Roma. What's yours?

LINGK Lingk. James Lingk.

ROMA James. I'm glad to meet you. (*They shake hands*) I'm glad to meet you, James.

Glengarry Glen Ross – *David Mamet (Stage version)*

▌ **GLOSSARY** ▌

gimlet *a drink made of gin, lime and water*

a couple *two*

2 Work in small groups. What alternatives do you know for each of the three phrases that you have underlined?

**ALTERNATIVE
VERSIONS**

[cassette icon] Listen to the two alternative versions of a similar situation involving two men called Buxton and Roberts. Which one of these four sentences describes the first conversation and which one describes the second conversation?

1 Buxton already knows Roberts' name but this is the first time they have met.
2 Buxton and Roberts are old friends.
3 Buxton introduces himself to Roberts in a formal way.
4 Buxton and Roberts are meeting for the second time.

GREETING PHRASES   📼 Now read these questions, listen again and write the answers in the right-hand column. Check your answers with others in the class.

Which phrase is a formal way to introduce yourself?	
Which phrase is the answer to 'How do you do'?	
Which phrase do you say when you know someone's name but you haven't met them before?	
Which phrase is a polite way of asking for someone's name?	

HAVE YOU MET ...?   👥 Introduce yourselves in the following three situations.

▮ **A** You are sitting in a bar. **B** sits down at the next chair.
▮ **A** and **B** You are guests at a formal reception at an embassy.
▮ **A** You are on a business trip to another country. **B** is waiting for you at the airport.

... AND INTRODUCING OTHER PEOPLE

This is the script for part of a scene from the Hollywood movie, *Wall Street*. Bud Fox is introducing his father to several people at the start of a meeting.

1 Read the scene below and answer these questions.

1 How many people does Bud Fox introduce?
2 Which person has met Bud's father before?
3 Who does Bud Fox introduce in the most formal way?

BUD	Dad, I think you know Dr Wilmer.
DAD	Since before you were born. How are you?
BUD	Toni Carpenter, Flight Attendant.
CARPENTER	How are you?
BUD	And I want you to meet Mr Gekko.
GEKKO	Hi, Mr Fox, it's a pleasure to meet you.
BUD	His Attorney, Mr Soul.
DAD	How are you doing?

▮ **GLOSSARY** ▮
attorney   *lawyer*

Bud Fox (Charlie Sheen) introduces his father, played by Martin Sheen, to some of his business associates

2 Underline the two phrases that Bud uses to introduce people in the scene.

3 In small groups, make a list of other ways of introducing people.

PLEASED TO MEET YOU!

Work in groups and take turns to introduce the other members of the group to each other. When introduced, greet each other in an appropriate way and carry on a conversation for a few minutes.

2 the **company**

Charles Handy

Company VOCABULARY

THE SHAMROCK ORGANISATION

The Irish management thinker, Charles Handy, believes that the traditional company is dying. In his book, *The Age of Unreason*, he says that today more and more people are working in a 'shamrock organisation'.

Read this description of the shamrock organisation. Where in the shamrock are you?

The first leaf of the shamrock represents the organisation's core workers. These employees are usually qualified professionals and managers. They work very long hours and, in return, receive high salaries and generous benefits.

Work that is not essential to the organisation goes to people in the second leaf of the shamrock. These people are normally self-employed and are specialists in certain kinds of work. They often sell their services to more than one organisation.

The third leaf of the shamrock is the flexible labour force – temporary and part-time workers. The organisation saves money because it only employs these people when it needs them.

ADVANTAGES AND DISADVANTAGES

1 Compare the shamrock organisation with a traditional company. What are the advantages and disadvantages of a shamrock organisation for the following?

	ADVANTAGE	DISADVANTAGE
For the company ...		
For the core workers ...		
For the self-employed people ...		
For the flexible labour force ...		

2 Compare your lists with others in the class.

WORD FAMILIES

1 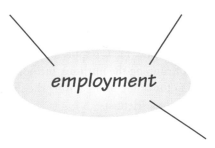 How many words on these two pages can you find that are derived from this word.

employment

Can you think of any other words in this word family?

2 Now, build word families for each of these words. (You can find some related words on these two pages.)

special   a representative
an organiser   *to manage*

3 Compare your answers with others in the group.

A COMPANY REORGANISATION

A traditional oil company has decided to reorganise as a shamrock organisation in order to cut costs. Work in small groups and discuss these points. In each case, give your reasons.

1 Which of these jobs should you keep in the core?

accountant   computer programmer   lawyer
geologist   chief executive officer
personnel manager   company doctor   secretary

What other jobs should be in the core?

2 Is it better to use self-employed workers or a flexible labour force to do the non-core jobs?

3 Which of these functions should you keep in the core?

cleaning   strategic planning   training   sales
catering   administration
travel bookings

4 Which non-core functions should be done by self-employed workers and which by a flexible force?

THE SHAMROCK AND YOU

1 How close is your company to a shamrock organisation? Describe the ways in which your companies use core workers, self-employed workers and a flexible labour force.

2 In the business world, which of the three groups do you think is growing most quickly? Give reasons for your opinion.

GRAMMAR REVIEW

A JOB DESCRIPTION

Julian Lee is the general manager of a nuclear research institute. He is responsible for all aspects of running the institute, including managing the staff and organising the finances, but he is not a scientist.

BNC
NUCLEAR RESEARCH DIVISION

Julian Lee *General manager*

West House, High Street, Leeds, LE1 4HB
Tel 0113–245 6267   Fax 0113–243 3123
e-mail julian.lee.@.bnc.res.

1 Which of the tasks below do you think he has to do and which of them doesn't he have to do?

	WHAT DOES HE HAVE TO DO?	WHAT DOESN'T HE HAVE TO DO?
find new uses for radioactive material		
recruit new staff		
repair the equipment		
conduct performance appraisals		
prepare the budgets		
check health and safety procedures		
sell the institute's ideas in foreign markets		

2 🗣 Compare your answers with a partner.

3 ▭ Check your answers with Julian Lee's own description of his job.

PRACTICE 1   🗣 Take turns to ask and answer questions about your obligations in your jobs. Start by asking about a few of the tasks above (e.g. Do you have to prepare the budgets?), then invent your own questions.

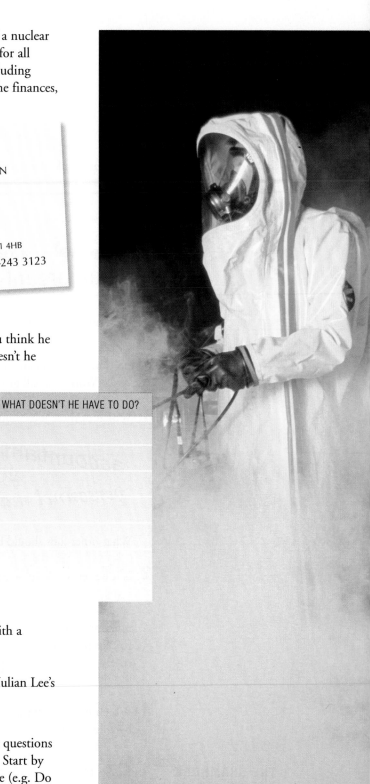

SAFETY PROCEDURES

On the tape, you'll hear Julian Lee talking to a new member of staff about health and safety procedures in the rest area of his institute. As you listen, answer these questions.

1 What do you have to do?
2 What don't you have to do?
3 What mustn't you do?

CHECK

You use *have to* or *must* to talk about an obligation, although, when talking about responsibilities, *have to* is more common, e.g.

You have to lock this door every evening at 18.00.

The negative form, *don't have to* is used when you don't have an obligation, e.g.

You don't have to arrive before 09.30.

But you use the negative form *mustn't* to talk about an obligation <u>not</u> to do something, e.g.

You mustn't drink alcohol during working hours.

For more on these grammar points, turn to page 135

'DON'T HAVE TO' OR 'MUSTN'T'?

Now answer these questions.

1 There is a leak of radiation at the laboratory. What do you say?
   a You mustn't go into the laboratory.
   b You don't have to go into the laboratory.
2 You are helping a new researcher at the institute. What do you say about her lunch hour?
   a You mustn't have lunch at the same time every day.
   b You don't have to have lunch at the same time every day.
3 You want to leave some important papers on the floor in your office overnight. What do you tell the cleaner?
4 It's the end of the day and your secretary wants to go home. You give him/her some typing to do which is not urgent. What do you say to him/her?

PRACTICE 2

Talk about working conditions at your company (or at a company you know well). Tell each other about the following: dress code, smoking policy, working hours, alcohol policy, lunch times.

doing **business** *Meetings*

PREPARING FOR A MEETING

Michael Crichton is one of America's best-selling novelists. This is what he writes about how to behave at a meeting with a Japanese person.

1 🎭 Read the description and answer these questions about the text. What does Michael Crichton say about ...

1 ... the best way to greet a Japanese person?
2 ... being direct?
3 ... your body language?

'It'll help to be formal. Stand straight and keep your suit jacket buttoned at all times. If they bow to you, don't bow back – just give a little head nod. A foreigner will never master the etiquette of bowing. Don't even try.

When you start to deal with the Japanese, remember that they don't like to negotiate. They find it too confrontational. In their own society, they avoid it wherever possible.

Control your gestures. Keep your hands at your sides. The Japanese find big arm movements threatening. Speak slowly. Keep your voice calm and even.'

Rising Sun, *Michael Crichton*

This extract comes from the novel, Rising Sun. *It tells the story of a police investigation into a murder at the head office of a Japanese company in the USA. It later became a film starring Wesley Snipes and Sean Connery.*

2 🎭 What advice would you give to someone who is preparing for their first meeting in your country/countries?

KINDS OF MEETING

Here are five situations which you could describe as 'meetings'.

1 Match each situation to one of the five meetings in the box.

1 Several people trying to think of new ideas
2 Two people talking in a corridor
3 One person giving several other people information about a new project
4 A boss talking to someone about his or her recent performance
5 Several people having a regular meeting to discuss the way a project is developing.

a progress review

a brainstorming

an appraisal

a chat   **a briefing**

2 🎭 Talk about the sorts of meeting that you have in your jobs.

FORMAL AND INFORMAL MEETINGS

1 Which of the meetings on page 20 do you think are normally formal and which are normally informal?

2 Work in small groups. Which of these things do you expect at a formal meeting and which at an informal meeting? Give examples for some of the meetings in the list above.

an agenda   matters arising   AOB   coffee

a chairperson   an objective   a time limit

minutes   any other business   briefing documents

3 Listen to the the meeting. Tick the items in the box which they mention. Do you think that this is a formal or an informal meeting?

MEETING PHRASES

1 Here are six phrases that you heard in the meeting. Write them in the correct boxes.

What do you mean by that?	Are there any questions?
We're here today to sort out this mess.	Can I say something here?
Let's get down to business.	Can you repeat what you said about the money?

To signal the start	
To introduce the objective	
To ask for questions	
To ask for clarification	
To ask for repetition	
To interrupt	

2 Think of other appropriate phrases for the above table.

3 Listen again to the meeting on the recording and answer these questions.
1 What do they have to decide at the meeting?
2 What's the time limit for the meeting?
3 How much money are they going to lose?
4 Who is taking minutes?

MEETING ROLES 1

Work in small groups and have a series of short meetings. Take turns to be chairperson.

The chairperson should choose the subject of the meeting and decide on things like a time limit, agenda, minutes, etc. At the beginning of each meeting he or she should do the following:
1 Signal the start.
2 Introduce the objective.
3 Mention issues such as agenda, time limit as appropriate.
4 Ask for questions.

Others in the group should interrupt, ask for clarification, repetition, etc. as appropriate.

doing **business** *Discussion in meetings*

A COMPANY PROBLEM

Read this problem, then work in small groups and, briefly, discuss these questions.

1 What do you think – should employers do more to protect staff?
2 What solutions to the problem can you think of?

❙ GLOSSARY ❙

an assault *a physical attack*
a retail employee *a shop worker*
shoplifters *people who steal goods from shops*

It is estimated that there is an assault on a retail employee during every minute of every day. Shoplifters make up 62% of this total – the rest are mostly drunks, drug addicts or angry customers. But few companies have any kind of strategy to deal with violence in the workplace. Should employers do more to protect staff against violence?

Management Today, May 1997

A DISCUSSION

1 🔲 You will hear part of a meeting to discuss the problem above. Listen and answer these questions.

1 What three suggestions are made to solve the problem?
2 Who do you think has the strongest opinion?
3 Which of these phrases does this person use to introduce his/her opinion?

> Have you thought about ... ?   Why don't you ... ?   I think you should ...

2 👥 What other phrases do you know to introduce an opinion?

MAKING YOUR POINT

1 🔲 Now you'll hear three extracts from the same discussion. The speakers express the same opinions as before, but they use different phrases to introduce them. Work in small groups and discuss these points:

1 Does the use of a different phrase make their opinions seem weaker, stronger or no different from the original meeting?
2 When you're giving an opinion, which do you think is more important – the words you choose or the way you choose to say them?

2

A Use one of the phrases above to introduce the same opinion in two (or more) different ways – in other words, express your opinion using your tone of voice, not the words themselves.

B Try to guess which is supposed to be the stronger opinion and which is the weaker.

Swap roles.

ASKING FOR AN OPINION

1 Listen again to the whole of the meeting about violence in the workplace. Make a note of the three phrases that Harriet (the chairperson) uses to ask for opinions.

2 Make a list of other similar phrases that you know.

MEETING ROLES 2

Work in groups of around 3–4 people and have meetings to discuss solutions to these two business problems.

Groups should take a few minutes to read the problem under discussion. Then, somebody should act as chairperson and begin the meeting in the way described in *Meeting roles 1* (in *Doing business 1*).

1

Time for a smoke break?

The anti-smoking lobby continues. In the early 1980s less than 5% of UK companies had a policy towards smoking. Today, according to ASH (Action on Smoking and Health) nine out of 10 major companies have some code of practice on smoking in the workplace. But more than 25% of Britain's adults continue to smoke, so what attitude should the other employers take? Should they try to accommodate the needs of smokers as well as non-smokers? Or should they ban smoking completely?

Management Today, *June 1996*

2

Travel sick blues

Business travellers are making up to 15% more trips than a year ago. The constant time zone changes, time wasted in transit and frequent delays wear down many. What can the tired executive do about the problems of business travel? And under what circumstances can he or she simply say 'no' when asked to go on yet another trip?

Management Today, *May 1997*

focus

Hanson

HANSON'S
EMPIRE

· · · · · · · · · · · · · · ·

Between the early 1960s and the mid 1990s, two British businessmen, James Hanson and Gordon White, built a global business conglomerate with a value of over £10.5 billion. During that period they bought over 40 companies in the UK and the USA.

However, Gordon White died in August 1995 and a few months later the 74-year-old James Hanson decided to break up their empire.

Hanson wanted to divide his conglomerate into four groups of companies.

James Hanson

1 On the opposite page are details of eight of Hanson's major companies. You don't need to understand every word in the texts, but find the answers to these questions as quickly as possible:

1 Which company owns power stations?
2 Which company is interested in continental Europe?
3 Which company's main customers are in the paint and paper industries?
4 Which company had a flat turnover last year?
5 Which company is the world's biggest private coal miner?
6 What are aggregates?
7 Which company is based in California?
8 Which company produces polyethylene?
9 Which company has nearly no international business?
10 Which company is interested in power generation in Asia?

2 Now hold a meeting to decide what is the best way to divide the conglomerate into four groups of companies. Give your reasons. (N.B. You don't need to make four groups of two – a 'group' could be just one company.)

3 When you've reached a decision, compare your ideas with what James Hanson actually did (see page 124). What are the principles behind James Hanson's decision? How are they different from yours?

1

Company name: SCM
Location: USA
Main product: Titanium oxide
(a chemical used to make things white)
Main customers: the paint and paper industries
Sales: £531 million
Future plans: to increase production capacity by
22% before 2000

5

● EASTERN GROUP

The Eastern Group has a number of power stations in the UK and makes most of its profits from electricity distribution in the south-east of England. It is also the UK's fourth largest supplier of gas. Eastern's management would like to develop international interests.

Profits last year: £245 million

2

Imperial Tobacco

Imperial Tobacco is number two in the British cigarette market. Its operating profits are £350 million from sales of £780 million and it will soon have new factories that will make it even more efficient. But these profits are nearly all in the British market; it has almost no international business.

6

ARC

ARC is the second largest producer of aggregates (rock, sand and gravel) in the UK. It is also second in coated stone for road construction. Despite a difficult construction market last year, ARC increased operating profits from £69 million to £84 million on flat turnover of £563 million.

3

Company name: Cornerstone
Location: California, USA
Main product: aggregates
(rock, sand & gravel)
Turnover: £930 million
Profit: £50 million

7

PEABODY

Peabody is the world's largest private sector coal miner and a leading US distributor of propane gas. Hanson's accounts show that St Louis-based Peabody had a difficult time last year. While profits rose from £149 million to £215 million, the underlying trend was down. Peabody is currently interested in power generation projects in Asia.

4

HANSON BRICK

Hanson Brick has about 30% of the UK brick market. Last year it increased its profits from £23 million to £38 million despite the difficult housing market. It is now turning its attention to continental Europe.

8

● QUANTUM

Quantum is an American chemical company that specialises in plastics, in particular, polyethylene products. Last year it made operating profits of 30% on sales of £1.4 billion. However, it operates in a very unstable market and results will probably not be as good over the next few years.

Sources: The Financial Times, 31.1.96
The Economist, 3.2.96

Visitors

FIRST IMPRESSIONS

1 When you receive a visitor at your company, which of the following do you do?

▌ hang his/her coat up

▌ offer tea or coffee

▌ exchange business cards

▌ offer something to eat

2  Compare your answers. What else would you normally do at the beginning of a meeting with a visitor to your company?

OFFERS AND REQUESTS

This is a scene from the film *Other People's Money*. Garfield, a financier, and his secretary, Harriet, are starting a meeting with a businesswoman called Mrs Sullivan.

1 Look at the script below and underline the following:

1 the phrase to ask permission

2 the phrase to request something

3 the two phrases used to make an offer.

2 Compare your answers.

GARFIELD	Do you want a cup of coffee? A cup of tea? A glass of water?
SULLIVAN	You needn't be sociable, Mr Garfield.
GARFIELD	Harriet, can I have a cup of coffee?
HARRIET	Yes, sir.
GARFIELD	Do you mind if I smoke?
SULLIVAN	I'd like to tell you why I'm here.
GARFIELD	Good. Shoot.
SULLIVAN	I'm here to plead for our company. I want to talk to you about hopes and dreams, traditions.
GARFIELD	Would you care for a doughnut, Mrs Sullivan?

▌ **GLOSSARY** ▌

shoot	*continue*
to plead	*to ask for help*

Other People's Money *is a comedy in which Danny Devito plays a tough New York financier.*

3 Look again at the script and answer these questions.

1 How would you describe Garfield's relationship with Mrs Sullivan? Choose one or more adjectives from this box.

| friendly | unfriendly | formal | informal | tense | relaxed |

Give reasons for your choice of adjective(s).

2 Which of the two phrases that Garfield uses to make an offer is more formal?

4 Now adapt the phrases you have underlined for the following situations:

1 During a meeting you want to open the window.
2 You notice that your guest's coffee cup is empty.
3 You want a glass of water.

5 What else can you say in these situations? Work in groups and try to think of three phrases for each situation in exercise 4.

BEING POLITE   In the script, Mrs Sullivan ignores Garfield's questions.

1 What would she say, to be polite to him? Fill in the gaps.

> Do you want a cup of coffee? A cup of tea? A glass of water?
>
> _____
>
> Do you mind if I smoke?
>
> _____
>
> Would you care for a doughnut?
>
> _____

2 In your version of the conversation, which responses are positive and which are negative?

3 Now rewrite the conversation again, changing positive responses to negative ones and negative responses to positive ones.

WELCOMING ROLES   Have conversations for the following three situations.

▮ **A** You are a visitor at **B**'s company. The meeting room is very hot and the windows are shut. You are both thirsty and there is no water on the table.
▮ **B** You are a visitor at **A**'s company. You are both at a buffet lunch. Offer/Ask for cold meat, salad, bread, wine and fruit juice, responding as appropriate.
▮ Take turns to start a normal meeting with a visitor at your company.

3 money

Financial VOCABULARY

A SUCCESSFUL INVESTOR? What do you think makes a successful investor? Rank the things in the box from 1 to 7. Add any other things which you think are important.

a long-term strategy	good luck	courage	caution
quick thinking	good timing	good advice	

THE TOP FOUR The UK's *Independent* newspaper of 19.9.96 described the four men below as the world's most successful investors.

 Read the profiles and decide which of the above qualities were most important for each of these four men.

NOTE
bn = billion
m = million

Perhaps the most outstanding investor of recent times is WARREN BUFFET of Omaha, Nebraska. He started in 1956 with $100 and is today one of the world's richest men, with a personal fortune of more than $8.5 bn. He did it by careful, long-term investment in simple, mass-market companies. It's a strategy that has <u>outperformed</u> the Dow Jones industrial average in every year since 1956.

SIR JOHN TEMPLETON turned a £10,000 investment in 1954 into more than £300 m. He did this as a result of "investing at the time of maximum <u>pessimism</u>" – in other words, moving against current investment fashions. He bought when stock markets were lowest and sold when they rose.

SIR JAMES GOLDSMITH is worth around £1.15 bn. He made his money as an <u>asset stripper</u>, but he kept it because of his sense of timing. He anticipated the financial <u>crash</u> of 1974, the boom of the early 1980s and the great stock market crash of 1987.

GEORGE SOROS'S Curaçao-based Quantum Fund has produced a return of almost 35 per cent a year over 26 years, the greatest growth fund in history. A <u>stake</u> of £1,000 invested with Soros in 1969 would be worth £2.15 m today. Most famously, Soros made £1 bn by selling sterling just before it was <u>devalued</u> (after leaving the European exchange rate mechanism), and then buying it back.

A FEW DEFINITIONS   Look again at the texts and match the underlined words to these definitions:

1 reduced in value

2 has done better than

3 thinking that whatever happens will be bad

4 money that is risked in a business

5 a sudden collapse

6 a person who buys an unsuccessful company, sells its most valuable parts and then closes it down.

GOOD TIMES ...
BAD TIMES ...

1 Look at the list of words and phrases on the right. Which are associated with success and which are associated with failure?

SUCCESS	FAILURE

boom   expansion   decline   crash   growth   slump   recession   golden age   bull market   bear market

2 Add any other words or phrases that you can think of.

3 Mark which of these sentences are true and which are false.

1 During the slump of the 1930s, there was a lot of unemployment and high inflation in many countries.

2 The decline of the Japanese economy since World War Two has been extraordinary.

3 The 1950s was a golden age for the American economy.

4 The oil crisis of the 1970s led to a period of expansion for most Western countries.

5 The 1987 stock market boom was the worst financial disaster for many years.

6 Investment bankers made huge amounts of money during the bear market of the mid 1990s.

4 Replace one word in each of the false sentences with words from the list above to make true sentences.

5 Now use some of the words and phrases to talk about the following:

▌ the economy of your country over the past twenty years

▌ the history of your company.

SHARES AND CURRENCIES

1 Build two vocabulary networks around these topics:

1 currency

2 shares.

Use the words and phrases on the right and then add any others that you know.

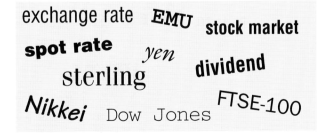

exchange rate   EMU   stock market   spot rate   yen   sterling   dividend   Nikkei   Dow Jones   FTSE-100

2 Work in small groups and explain the meanings of the words and phrases.

INVESTMENT AND YOU   You have £1,000 to invest. Look again at the four successful investors opposite. Who would you give your money to? Explain why.

G R A M M A R   R E V I E W

GORDON GEKKO'S FIRST DEAL

In this scene from the film *Wall Street*, Gordon Gekko describes his first successful business deal.

A Do not read the text. Look at the left-hand column and put the verbs into the correct form to ask six questions.

B Read the text.

Now, **A** should ask and **B** should answer the questions about Gordon Gekko's first deal.

1 What (he buy)?
2 When (he buy) it?
3 How long (he keep) it?
4 How much profit (he make)?
5 How (he feel) about it at that time?
6 How (he feel) about it now?

In Oliver Stone's film, Wall Street, Michael Douglas plays Gordon Gekko, a financial trader with just one interest in life – money!

You see that building? I bought that building ten years ago – my first real estate* deal. Sold it two years later, made an $800,000 profit. It was better than sex. At that time I thought that was all the money in the world. Now, it's a day's pay.

* real estate (US) = property (UK)

PRACTICE 1   What was your most (or least) successful deal? It can be something from your business career or your personal life (e.g. buying and selling a car). Ask and answer questions about it.

CHECK

We use the past simple tense to talk about a finished action in the past which happened at a definite time.

I bought that building ten years ago.

The negative form is:

I didn't buy that building ten years ago.

And the question form is:

When did you buy that building?

▌ *For more on the past simple, turn to page 139* ▌

THE PAUL REICHMANN STORY

Canary Wharf

Paul Reichmann

World Financial Center in front of the World Trade Center

1 Listen to the story of one of the greatest property developers – Paul Reichmann and his company, Olympia & York.

2 Number these events in the order in which they happened.

Work begins on Canary Wharf in East London.

Paul Reichmann joins the family business.

His company collapses with debts of $20 billion.

He builds the World Financial Center in New York.

He works on religious and educational projects in North Africa. *1*

He takes control of Canary Wharf again.

The Reichmanns become the largest owners of property in New York.

3 Put the verbs in the story above into the correct tense – in the correct order.

4 Now listen to the Paul Reichmann story again and answer these questions.

1 What was happening to the London property market when Olympia & York collapsed?

2 What was Paul doing when his brothers started Olympia & York?

3 What was Margaret Thatcher's government trying to do in East London in the mid 80s?

4 What was happening in New York when Olympia & York bought the Canary Wharf site?

CHECK

Two main tenses are used to tell the Paul Reichmann story:

- the past continuous, e.g. *property markets were experiencing a slump*
- the past simple, e.g. *the company collapsed*

Can you explain why these different tenses are used?

▌ *For more on the past continuous and past simple, turn to page 138* ▌

PRACTICE 2

A Think of at least five questions to ask B about the Paul Reichmann story.

B Read the tapescript of the Paul Reichmann story and get ready to answer A's questions.

Now ask and answer the questions.

doing **business** *Figures*

DATES, ODDS AND PI

1 Write down the following in figures:

Twenty-sixth of the twelfth ninety-four	_____	Ten to twelve	_____
Nineteen eighty-nine	_____	Six to one	_____
Two and three-quarter billion	_____	Thirty love	_____
Three point one four two eight five	_____	Five-sixteenths	_____

2 Match each of the figures to one of these:

3 Write down a list containing at least five different kinds of figures (e.g. dates, sums of money, fractions, years, times). Take turns to dictate your lists to each other and compare your lists with the originals.

> **gambling odds**   *a tennis score*
> **the time**   a year
> *a small measurement in inches*
> **a birthday**   Pi
> Bill Gates' wealth in dollars in the mid-90s

STRESS

When you listen, it's easy to confuse 60 with 16 or 40 with 14. One way to tell the difference is to listen for the stress.

1 Put a mark above the parts of these words which are stressed and then listen to the tape.

thirty   thirteen   forty   fourteen

2 Listen to the next part of the tape and write down the sequence of figures that you hear.

3 Write down a sequence of numbers like 13 ... 30 ... 14 ... 40 and then dictate them to your partner.

SOME ACCOUNTING TERMS

Look at the two simplified accounting statements opposite. Find the terms which mean the following:

1 what a company owns _____
2 the total amount of sales _____
3 what a company owes _____
4 the profit made by the normal activities of a business _____
5 the goods which a business intends to sell to its customers. _____

ACCOUNTING ROLES

1

A Look at the incomplete balance sheet. Ask B for the missing information.
B Turn to page 124 and look at the balance sheet. Answer A's questions.

2

B Look at the incomplete profit and loss account. Ask A for the missing information.
A Turn to page 125 and look at the profit and loss account. Answer B's questions.

BALANCE SHEET AT MARCH 31

	£
FIXED ASSETS	
Land	....
Buildings	20,000
	50,000
CURRENT ASSETS	
Stock	....
Debtors	....
Cash	5,000
	50,000
CREDITORS	
(falling due within 12 months)	....
NET CURRENT LIABILITIES	(40,000)
TOTAL ASSETS LESS CURRENT LIABILITIES	....
CAPITAL	....

PROFIT AND LOSS ACCOUNT FOR THE YEAR TO MARCH 31

	This year	Last year
TURNOVER	200,000	....
Cost of sales	....	180,000
Gross profit	....	60,000
Administration costs	15,000	....
OPERATING PROFIT	....	40,000

2 doing business *The language of graphs*

BLACK MONDAY 1   Listen to the radio news report on the great stock market crash on 'Black Monday' and answer these questions.

1 What date was 'Black Monday'?
2 How much money was lost on the London market?
3 By how many points did the Dow Jones index fall?
4 What percentage was this?
5 When was the previous great stock market crash?
6 By how much did the market fall then?

2 Compare your answers and check by listening again.

to stay the same   to recover
to soar   to dip   to peak
to increase   to stabilise
to hit the bottom   to decrease
to fall   to plunge   to rise

UPS AND DOWNS 1 Complete the table with these verbs. Add any other appropriate verbs that you know.

UP	DOWN	NO CHANGE
to soar		

2 Which of the verbs do you think best describe points 1 to 10 of this graph?

3 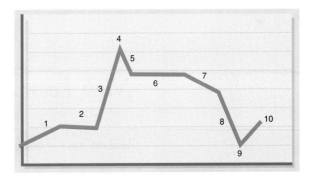 Listen again to the report on Black Monday and tick the verbs which the newsreader uses.

SOUND AND SPELLING '-ED'

The final **-ed** of regular verbs in the past simple tense is pronounced in three different ways.

1 🔊 Listen to the pronunciation of the three verbs in the column below and repeat what you hear.

/d/	/t/	/ɪd/
closed	increased	lasted

2 Now decide how to pronounce the final **-ed** of these verbs and write them in the appropriate column of the table above.

3 👥 Compare your pronunciation of the verbs.

4 🔊 Check your answers.

crashed   *decided*   ***invested***

collapsed   intended   **peaked**

stabilised   slumped

recovered   plunged   predicted   **soared**

THE DOW JONES INDEX

👥 Here is a graph of the Dow Jones index on Black Monday. Use some of the language on this page to describe what happened.

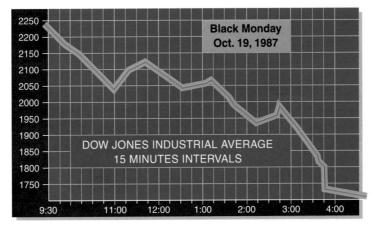

focus

Nick Leeson and the collapse of Barings

Read the story of Nick Leeson. Stop where indicated and discuss the questions in small groups.

Nick Leeson

1 Is it normal for large, well-established companies to collapse as the result of one person's actions?
■ If not, why not? And if so, why?
■ Can you give another example of a similar event?

2 When a fairly junior member of a company is suddenly very successful, what do you think should be the management's most appropriate response? Explain why.
a delight
b interest
c curiosity
d suspicion

> *Taking a futures position is a 50-50 gamble. There were days when I could lose £25–£30 million, there were days when I made £50 million.*
>
> **Nick Leeson**
> The Times 11.9.95

3 Is Nick Leeson right – are the financial markets a gambling casino? Or are they a place for careful, responsible investment? What is your view?

4 What do you think was the best thing for Leeson to do in this situation?
a Contact his bosses and explain everything.
b Take a long holiday.
c Continue 'gambling' in the hope that he would win the money back again.
Can you think of any other options?

5 Who do you think was really responsible for this banking collapse: Nick Leeson or his bosses?

6 What kind of punishment do you think they deserved? Discuss the options in this table.

	LEESON	HIS BOSSES
None		
Dismissal		
A fine		
A prison sentence		

7 Do you think that Leeson and his bosses were fairly treated? Give your reasons.

The Kobe earthquake killed over 5000 people.

NICK LEESON AND THE COLLAPSE OF BARINGS

Nick Leeson is led away by police officers.

ON FEBRUARY 26 1995 the world was shocked by the news that Britain's oldest bank, Barings, had collapsed. People were even more surprised when they learnt that it was due to the actions of just one man – a young trader called Nick Leeson.

Leeson had started working at Barings' Singapore office in 1992, when he was 25 years old. Using the bank's money, he bought and sold derivatives* contracts – like futures and options – at SIMEX, the Singapore Monetary Exchange. This can be a very risky business, but Barings thought it knew what it was doing.

STOP

Go to question 1

Leeson quickly became the star of the Singapore office and its profits from derivatives trading grew dramatically. His bosses in London were delighted. But they didn't know the full story. In fact, while his huge profits appeared in the official reports, he was hiding his losses in a secret account. And his losses were much, much bigger!

The truth was that Nick Leeson had never behaved like an ordinary trader. He saw the financial markets as a gambling casino and, just like a losing gambler, he believed that he would win in the end. So, towards the end of 1994 he decided to solve his problems by making a very big gamble.

STOP

Go to questions 2 and 3

Leeson thought that the Tokyo stock market would remain fairly stable for the next few months. He knew that he could make a good profit from this situation by selling a special kind of option contract – so he sold

thousands and thousands of them. But, unfortunately for Leeson, Japan was entering a very unstable period.

On 17 January 1995 a huge earthquake hit the industrial city of Kobe. In response, the Tokyo stock market plunged. Leeson's gamble had gone badly wrong and Barings had lost a huge sum of money.

STOP

Go to question 4

Leeson didn't stop gambling. He believed that by spending an enormous amount of his bank's money, he could control the market and save his position. But he was wrong. By February 23, he had lost more than £300 million and the game was over. The following day he and his wife flew to Malaysia for a holiday.

Back in London, Leeson's bosses realised what had happened. Day by day, as the losses grew, it became clear that Barings was bankrupt. On March 6 it was sold to a Dutch bank for just £1.

STOP

Go to questions 5 and 6

On March 2 1995 Leeson was arrested by German police at Frankfurt airport on his way from Malaysia to the UK. He was later sentenced to six and a half years in a Singaporean jail. On May 1 of the same year, twenty-one members of Barings' senior staff resigned or were sacked by the new owners.

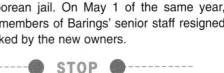

STOP

Go to question 7

NOTE

* Derivatives contracts are financial contracts which get (or 'derive') their value from the value of something else.

Breaking the ice

social skills

DO YOU COME HERE OFTEN?

1 At your office, you meet a visitor. Here are five things that you could find out about this person. Think of two ways of asking about each thing. Compare your questions.

Name _____ _____

Home town _____ _____

Reason for visit _____ _____

Length of stay _____ _____

Interests _____ _____

2 Listen to the conversation. In which order do the five subjects occur? Are any of the questions new to you? If so, make a note of them.

3 What other questions would you ask a visitor to your company? What questions wouldn't you ask?

THE PLAYER

In the film *The Player*, Griffin Mill, an executive at a Hollywood film studio, goes into his boss's office and meets a visitor.

1 Read the script and complete this profile of the visitor.

PROFILE

NAME
....

HOME TOWN
....

REASON FOR VISIT
....

LENGTH OF STAY
....

INTERESTS
....

LEVENSON	Griffin, I don't think you've met Reg Goldman. You know his father, Harvey.
GRIFFIN	Yes, of course. Hi, Reg. You're from the bank in Boston.
LEVENSON	Reg is out here for a couple of weeks.
GRIFFIN	Great. Business or pleasure?
REG	A little of both, I hope.
LEVENSON	Reg is thinking of getting into production, Griffin.
GRIFFIN	Oh, really?
REG	It beats work, doesn't it, Griffin? I'd like to play some tennis though. Do you play tennis?
GRIFFIN	No, no, no. I'm too busy.

GLOSSARY

a couple of	*two*
it beats work	*it's better than work*

2 Work in small groups. Look at the script again and talk about these questions.

1 How does Griffin ask about the reason for Reg's visit?

2 Which phrase does Levenson use to introduce the reason for Reg's visit?

3 Think of at least two other subjects that Griffin could talk to Reg about. What questions should he ask to do this?

4 Think of at least two subjects that it is a good idea to avoid in this situation.

THREE ICE BREAKERS  Try the following role plays. In each case, both people should ask and answer questions.

▌**A** You are in a sauna in a hotel, when **B** walks in. You have not met before. Start a conversation.

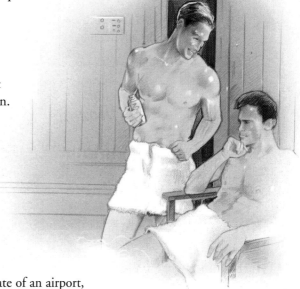

▌**A** You are at the departure gate of an airport, when you see **B**. You realise that you both work for the same multinational company. Have a two-minute conversation.

▌**A** During a business trip, you are sitting next to **B** in a ski lift, when it suddenly stops with the chair high above the ski slope. You think that **B** is attending the same conference as you. Have a three-minute conversation.

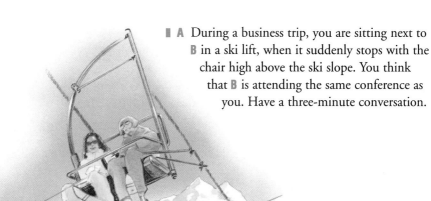

4 the **market**

Marketing VOCABULARY

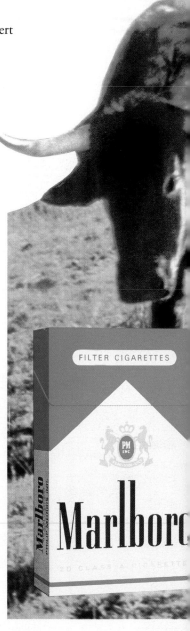

IMAGE

Marlboro is probably the most successful brand of cigarettes in the world. Its advertising and its image are famous in nearly every country.

But, what is special about Marlboro's image? Look at the Malboro advert and choose the two adjectives which you think describe it best.

glamorous   upmarket   *masculine*

luxurious   functional   downmarket

feminine   *caring*   simple   tough

What three other products could these adjectives describe?

POSITIONING

But Marlboro hasn't always had its current image, as the text opposite explains.

1 Before you read, look at the italicised words in the text and match them to these definitions.

- ▌ a person with an important job in the advertising business
- ▌ a series of advertisements
- ▌ to introduce a product to the market
- ▌ the group of people that the company wants to buy the product
- ▌ to make the product appeal to a different type of customer
- ▌ a short phrase

2 Now read the text and answer these two questions:

1 Who were Marlboro cigarettes originally for?
2 How successful was Marlboro before the 1950s?

3 Can you think of other products which have been repositioned? Here are two ideas. Explain how their images and target markets have changed.

1 Japanese cars (compare the 1960s with now)
2 running shoes (compare the 1970s with now)

SOUND AND SPELLING

In 1924, Philip Morris named Marlboro cigarettes after the English aristocrat, the Duke of Marlborough – but the company cut the final three letters from the name. That's because 'gh' or 'ugh' are sometimes silent in English, as in this case. In some cases, though, it's pronounced as 'f'.

1 How do you pronounce these words?

Marlborough *through*
tough rough cough
Edinburgh although

2 Compare your answers with those you hear.

THE TARGET MARKET

1 Discuss which of these groups of people you think this Marlboro advertisement appeals to. Rank them from 1 (high) to 5 (low).

CATEGORY	DEFINITION	RANK
yuppies	young urban professionals with a high income	
dinkies	couples with a double income and no kids	
the green market	people who are concerned about the environment	
blue collar workers	people who work with their hands	
ethnic minorities	people who are of a different race from the majority of people in a country	

2 Now discuss which target markets these brands are for: McDonald's, Disney, Mercedes-Benz, Levi's.

MARKETING AND YOU

Explain your answers to these questions:

1 What image does the most important product of your company (or one you know) have?

2 What is its target market?

3 How is it advertised?

Marlboro's image has changed dramatically since its early days. In fact, when the tobacco company, Philip Morris, *launched* Marlboro in 1924, its *target market* was women. Its advertising *slogan* said that it was 'Mild as May'. But it wasn't a great success and by the early 1950s it still had only around 1% of the total tobacco market. That was when the company asked the Chicago *advertising executive*, Leo Burnett, to *reposition* the product as a cigarette for men. He came up with an *advertising campaign* based on the image of a cowboy – and Marlboro's sales suddenly soared. Within a year it became the fourth best-selling brand in the USA; before long it was the biggest in the world.

G R A M M A R   R E V I E W

HAVE YOU EVER ...?

1 Look at these pairs of sentences. In each pair, put a line through the sentence which is *not* grammatically correct.

2 ● ● Compare your answers and explain your choices.

1 a Have you ever been to New York?
  b Have you been to New York last week?
2 a Have you seen Frank yesterday?
  b Did you see Frank yesterday?
3 a I haven't spoken to him since last year.
  b I didn't speak to him since last year.
4 a I am here for half an hour.
  b I have been here for half an hour.

█ CHECK

Notice that when you are talking about a period of time from the past up to the present, you use the present perfect.

Have you done that work yet?

When you are talking about a finished action at a definite time in the past, you use the past simple.

When did you do it?

█ *For more on this difference, see page 139* █

A LAUNCH CHECKLIST   ▭▭   On the recording, a marketing manager called Kate Philips talks to her boss about the preparations for a product launch.

1 As you listen, put a tick or cross in the first column, to show if she has done each task. If she has done a task, make a note of when she did it in the second column.

Launch checklist	Done?	When?
Book hotel		
Send out invitations		
Make travel arrangements		
Organise audio visual equipment		
Speak to Joan about catering		

2 ● ● Take turns to ask and answer questions about Kate's checklist, using one of these two patterns:

█ Has Kate booked the flights?
  No, she hasn't.

█ Has Kate booked the flights?
  Yes, she has.
  When did she book them?
  She booked them last week.

3 ● ● Why are different tenses used for the two questions in pattern 2?

**A PRODUCT LAUNCH
... BEFORE AND SINCE**

Read this story about the invention of one of the most common products for the office and put the verbs in brackets into the correct tenses.

THE POST-IT® STORY

Over the past twenty years, the yellow Post-It® note (become) [1] _has become_ a part of everyday office life around the world. But when the 3-M researcher, Dr Spencer Silver, (invent) [2] _____ the Post-It® note in 1970, his company's market research (show) [3] _____ that there (be) [4] _____ no market for such a product. In fact, 3-M (not launch) [5] _____ it until 1980. However, since then the product (be) [6] _____ an extraordinary success and (make) [7] _____ millions of dollars for the company.

PRACTICE

THE SEVEN MODERN WONDERS OF THE WORLD

In 1994, the magazine, *The Economist*, listed its seven modern wonders of the world (see pictures). Work in small groups and discuss these points, giving your reasons.

1 Which of these has had the biggest influence on our daily lives?
2 How has it changed our lives?
3 Which of these has had the biggest effect on business?
4 How has it changed business?
5 What other recent inventions have changed your life? What was life like before these products?

the hydrogen bomb

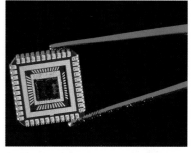

the microprocessor

the jumbo jet

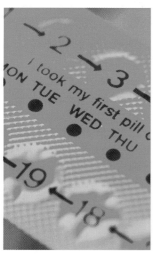

the contraceptive pill

the telephone network

*Tranquillity Base
(the American base on the moon)*

the off-shore oil platform

doing **business** *Making a proposal*

A PHOTOCOPIER SALESMAN

Patrick Allen is a salesman for a photocopier company. He visits Mr Jones, the owner of a small business.

1 Listen to their conversation and answer these questions.

1 What is Patrick offering free?

2 What is he trying to sell?

2 Now listen again and answer these questions.

1 Do you like Patrick Allen's style?

2 Why? Why not? Make a list of its good and bad points.

3 In Patrick Allen's situation, what would you do differently?

3 Compare your answers.

THE GODFATHER

The Godfather is a film about the New York Mafia. In the film, Sollazzo, a gangster, makes a business proposal to the man they call 'The Godfather', Don Corleone. Read the script and make a summary of the deal in the box at the top of the next page.

SOLLAZZO	Don Corleone. I need a man who has powerful friends. I need a million dollars in cash. I need, Don Corleone, those politicians that you carry in your pocket like so many nickels and dimes.
DON CORLEONE	What is the interest for my family?
SOLLAZZO	30%. In the first year, your end should be 3 … 4 million dollars. And then it would go up.
DON CORLEONE	And what is the interest for the Tattaglia family?
SOLLAZZO	I'll take care of the Tattaglias … out of my share.
DON CORLEONE	So I receive 30% for finance, political influence and legal protection. That's what you're telling me.
SOLLAZZO	That's right.
DON CORLEONE	Why did you come to me? Why do I deserve this generosity?
SOLLAZZO	If you consider a million dollars in cash just finance … ti salute, Don Corleone.

THE GODFATHER (PART 1)

▌ GLOSSARY ▌

nickels and dimes
  small American coins of not much value (5 c. and 10 c.)
your end
  your return

the Tattaglia family
  one of Don Corleone's big rivals

Marlon Brando plays Don Corleone, the boss of one of New York's top criminal organisations

WHAT DOES SOLLAZZO WANT?	WHAT IS HE OFFERING?

STRUCTURING A PROPOSAL

1 Now look again at the script and notice how the meeting is structured. In which order do these stages occur?

Don Corleone summarises.   Sollazzo says what he wants.

Don Corleone asks what is in it for him.   Sollazzo explains what he's offering.

2 Here is some of the language you can use for each of those four stages. Write the phrases and sentences in the appropriate boxes.

I need …   **Let's sum up …**   I'm offering …
What is the interest for me?
I'd like you to consider …   So this is the position …
I'm looking for …   *What's in it for me?*

If you're making an offer …

HOW TO SAY WHAT YOU WANT	HOW TO SAY WHAT YOU'RE OFFERING

And if you're listening to an offer …

HOW TO ASK ABOUT YOUR INTERESTS	HOW TO SUMMARISE THE DEAL

3 Add any other appropriate phrases that you know.

NEGOTIATING ROLES 1   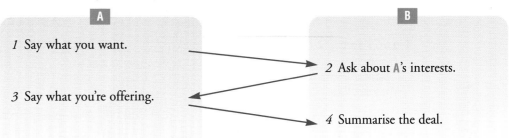   Use some of the phrases in the boxes to create your own version of Sollazzo and Don Corleone's meeting, following this structure:

A

1 Say what you want.

3 Say what you're offering.

B

2 Ask about **A**'s interests.

4 Summarise the deal.

2 doing business *Refusing and accepting*

SAYING NO

1 In small groups, look again at the script from *The Godfather* in *Doing Business 1*. In Don Corleone's position, if you wanted to refuse Sollazzo's proposal, which of these phrases would you use?

▌ I'm sorry, but that's out of the question.
▌ I must say no to you and I'll give you my reasons.
▌ I'm afraid we can't agree to that, but I hope to do business with you some other time.
▌ I need some time to think about that.

2 Which of the above phrases is the strongest form of refusal?

3 Which phrase suggests the possibility of compromise?

4 Think of other phrases that Don Corleone could use to refuse the offer.

A REFUSAL

Now read what Don Corleone actually says in the script below.

1 Underline the phrase that he uses to refuse the offer.

2 How does he 'soften' this refusal? Find at least two ways.

DON CORLEONE I said that I would see you because I heard that you were a serious man, to be treated with respect. But I must say no to you and I'll give you my reasons. It's true I have a lot of friends in politics, but they wouldn't be friendly very long if they knew my business was drugs and not gambling – which they regard as a harmless vice. But drugs is a dirty business ...

SOLLAZZO Don Corleone ...

DON CORLEONE It doesn't make a difference to me what a man does for a living, you understand. But your business is a little dangerous ...

▌ **GLOSSARY** ▌

a harmless vice
behaviour which is bad but not very dangerous

Don Corleone and Sollazzo shake hands at the end of their meeting

NEGOTIATING ROLES 2

> ▌ **A** Propose to **B** that you should go on holiday together to Spain for two weeks.
> **B** Refuse. (Think of at least one way of 'softening' this refusal.)
>
> ▌ **B** Propose to **A** that you should plan an office party to celebrate your manager's promotion.
> **A** Disagree.

SAYING YES

1 Some negotiators say that you should never accept the other person's first offer. Discuss. Why do you think they give this advice? Do you agree? (Where relevant, give examples from your own experience.)

2 Here are four ways of accepting a proposal. But which ones are unconditional acceptances and which allow space for a negotiation to develop?

> ▌ I like the sound of the idea.
> ▌ I think we have the basis of an understanding.
> ▌ That seems like a reasonable offer.
> ▌ OK, it's a deal.

3 How else can you accept a proposal?

FOUR ACCEPTANCES

You will hear four different ways of accepting an offer in the style of the Godfather. Which of these are definite acceptances and which leave room to negotiate? As you listen, tick the appropriate box.

	DEFINITE ACCEPTANCE	ROOM TO NEGOTIATE
Acceptance 1		
Acceptance 2		
Acceptance 3		
Acceptance 4		

NEGOTIATING ROLES 3

> ▌ **A** Find out what car **B** drives. Make an offer for it.
> **B** Respond as appropriate!
>
> ▌ **B** Propose that **A** should provide finance for a small business that you want to start (you choose which kind of business).
> **A** Respond as appropriate.

focus

Advertising

MELBOLTA 19C   Take a quick look at the advert below and decide:

1 What product is this advertising?
2 Which two adjectives best describe its image?
3 What kind of person is this product for?

THE CAMERA FOR PEOPLE WHO TRAVEL LIGHT

Have you ever wanted a camera that will capture the truly great moments in your life? Are you looking for a camera that's as tough and adventurous as you are?

The new Melbolta 19C has been specially designed for people who lead an active life. One of the smallest, lightest 35mm cameras ever produced, the 19C is protected by a tough shock-proof case that means you can take it virtually anywhere. Its unique sports grip allows you to point and shoot one-handed, while its automatic focus and zoom make sure that you take great pictures — even when your mind's on other things!

For more information about the Melbolta 19C, zoom in on your local Melbolta dealer.

We dare you!

MELBOLTA

Products at the edge

**FEATURES AND
BENEFITS**

Before advertisers write an advertisement, they look at the important facts about the product (its features). After this they think about how they will help the customer (its benefits). They then write the advert based on its benefits.

Here is a description of some of the Melbolta 19C's features.

Compare the list of features with the text of the advert opposite and discuss these points.

1 According to the advert, what benefits does each feature bring to customers?

2 What other benefits could each feature bring to customers?

**CREATE YOUR OWN
ADVERT**

Write an advert for this running shoe, based on this information sheet. Try using the approach suggested underneath.

1 Use the camera advert opposite as a model and follow this procedure:

1 *Target market*   Who do you want to sell these running shoes to? Think of at least five things about the kind of person who will buy them.
(e.g. Age? Sex? Income? Social class? Interests?)

2 *Image*   Now decide what kind of image you want to give to the shoes. Choose two adjectives to describe it and then think of a picture and a headline which will communicate this image immediately.

INFORMATION SHEET

MACQUARRIE 2000
RUNNING SHOE

De-odorising
insole

Fully
waterproof

Ankle
support

Special air
cushion sole

Designed by top Italian
fashion designer

3 *Create a need*   Think of the needs that this shoe will meet. Begin the advert with questions like:

Have you ever wanted ...?   Are you looking for ...?   Have you ever tried ...?

4 *Features and benefits*
Here are five benefits of these running shoes. Match the benefits to the features listed in the information sheet.

Your feet stay dry in wet weather   Your feet won't smell
You will look very fashionable   They are very comfortable
You won't injure your ankles

Now write a few sentences about the features and benefits of these shoes. You could use linking phrases like these:

FEATURE	means that ...	➡	BENEFIT
FEATURE	makes sure that ...	➡	BENEFIT
FEATURE	helps you to ...	➡	BENEFIT

5 *The call to action*   End your advert by asking the reader to take some action. Here are a few ideas:

For more information, write to this address ...
Visit your local sports shop today.
Buy them now, before it's too late.

2 Compare your adverts with those of others in the class.

Arrangements

social skills

LOOK AT IT THIS WAY

At the bottom of the page is an extract from a novel by Justin Cartwright called *Look at it this Way* – a comedy about business life in London.

In the extract, Victoria, a senior manager at an advertising agency phones Timothy Curtiz, who is the star of a TV commercial for a credit card called American Eagle. They discuss the arrangements for the filming of the commercial.

Read the extract and answer these questions.

1 Why does Timothy Curtiz want to make the arrangement for the filming as soon as possible?
2 When do they make an arrangement for?
3 Have they met before?
4 Why is it funny when Timothy Curtiz says 'Me too'?
5 Who will pay for their lunch?

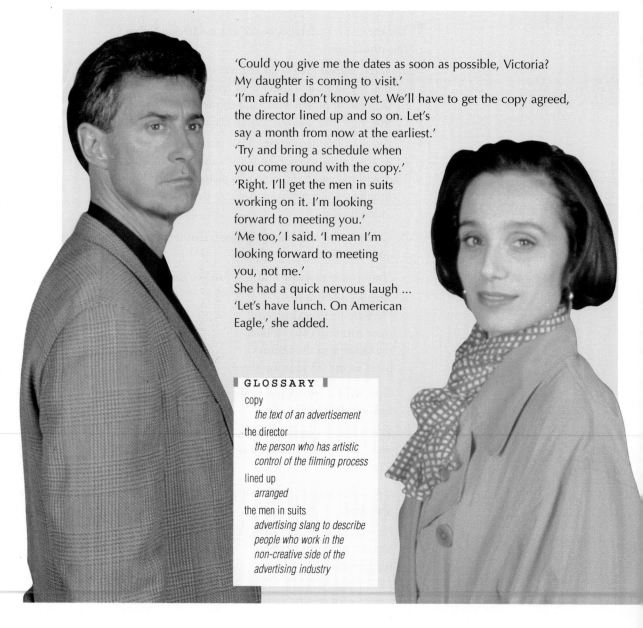

'Could you give me the dates as soon as possible, Victoria? My daughter is coming to visit.'
'I'm afraid I don't know yet. We'll have to get the copy agreed, the director lined up and so on. Let's say a month from now at the earliest.'
'Try and bring a schedule when you come round with the copy.'
'Right. I'll get the men in suits working on it. I'm looking forward to meeting you.'
'Me too,' I said. 'I mean I'm looking forward to meeting you, not me.'
She had a quick nervous laugh ...
'Let's have lunch. On American Eagle,' she added.

▌ GLOSSARY ▌

copy
  the text of an advertisement
the director
  the person who has artistic control of the filming process
lined up
  arranged
the men in suits
  advertising slang to describe people who work in the non-creative side of the advertising industry

MAKING AN ARRANGEMENT

1 Here are five pairs of sentences which have roughly the same meaning. Underline the five phrases in the text which have the same meanings as each of the pairs.

1 *Invitations*
  a Would you like to have lunch?
  b I would be honoured if you would have lunch with me.
2 *Arranging a time*
  a Tell me when it will be.
  b Can we fix a time?
3 *Suggesting a time*
  a How about a month from now?
  b I will not be available until a month from now.
4 *Being polite*
  a I anticipate our meeting with great pleasure.
  b It'll be great to meet you.
5 *Apologies*
  a I'm sorry. I can't tell you at the moment.
  b I apologise. No one has informed me.

2 Although both sentences in each pair have similar meanings, one sentence in each pair is an appropriate replacement for a sentence in the text; the other one isn't. Decide which sentence in each pair is an appropriate replacement and explain why. (Think about being too formal/too informal, polite/impolite, etc.)

3 You will hear an imaginary alternative version of the conversation in the book. Listen and compare your choices.

4 Think of at least one new sentence that you could add to each of the five categories above.

MAKING EXCUSES

If you can't agree to an arrangement, you normally need to make an excuse or you may sound impolite. Here are two common excuses:

I'm sorry, I'm away that day.   I'm afraid I can't make Tuesday.

How many more excuses can you think of?

ARRANGING ROLES

▌A Invite B to lunch tomorrow.
 B Accept the invitation.
 A Arrange a time.
 B Finish the conversation politely.

▌B Invite A for dinner tomorrow.
 A Explain that you can't go.
 B Suggest an alternative.
 A Respond appropriately.

5 management

Management VOCABULARY

TRUE OR FALSE?

Read the article opposite about Ford and then decide whether these statements are true or false.

1 Ford's new boss had spent his whole career at Ford.
2 Ford's American and European working practices were very similar.
3 The Ford 2000 plan had a lot of problems.
4 The main aim of the Ford 2000 plan was to cut costs.

**FORD 2000:
A SUMMARY**

When you've read about Ford 2000, look at this summary and replace the phrases in italics with words or phrases that are underlined in the text.

Ford is one of the world's most famous (1) *companies which operate in many different countries*. The project Ford 2000 was the (2) *coming together* of Ford's American and European operations. It involved great changes to the (3) *way that management is organised*, but it was more than just a change to the (4) *diagram of the company hierarchy*. Among other things, Ford hoped to get (5) *lower costs due to the increase in the scale of production*. The success of the project was partly due to the way that Ford's (6) *boss* communicated with the (7) *people who work for the company*.

1 _____   5 _____
2 _____   6 _____
3 _____   7 _____
4 _____

MANAGEMENT JARGON

1 Below are three pieces of management jargon which are used in the text. Try to explain what they mean.

globalisation   re-engineering   change management

2 Match them to the three definitions.

a way of completely reorganising a company which ignores both its past and present working practices
b introduction of new ideas and new working practices
c using the same products and methods in all parts of the world

3 What does the adjective 'Disneyesque' mean in the Ford 2000 text?

GLOBALISATION AND YOU

In small groups, discuss these points:

1 Do you think that this globalisation strategy has been a good idea for Ford?
2 Could a similar strategy be successful for your company (or one you know)?

MANAGEMENT BRIEF

Ford 2000

■ ONE AFTERNOON IN 1993, 15 senior managers from Ford's American and European divisions met in London. At the head of the table sat Alex Trotman, an Englishman who had just become the company's chairman and chief executive officer.

Mr Trotman is a perfect example of a company man. His entire career had been at Ford, starting in 1955 as a clerk at one of its factories near London. But he was about to change Ford dramatically.

At the meeting, Mr Trotman introduced the 'Ford 2000' initiative which brought together the company's European business (sales: $23 billion) with its North American one ($105 billion). Since each continent had separate management structures, products, factories and ways of doing things, it was, in effect, a huge corporate merger.

Full-scale globalisation, like this, is a difficult thing to do. In theory, a company can get rid of lots of unnecessary duplication and benefit from huge economies of scale. But, in practice, things can easily go wrong.

One of the reasons that Ford 2000 went relatively smoothly was because Mr Trotman worked hard to involve his workforce. In a video shown to all Ford's 320,000 employees, he explained that Ford 2000 was not just a re-drawing of an organisation chart, but a whole new way of working. The aim was not just to cut costs and increase efficiency, but to produce cars to delight their customers.

Perhaps this seems like a Disneyesque approach to re-engineering a major multinational. But, by 1996, Ford had become a very different organisation.

How far have Ford's high hopes been realised? As an exercise in change management, Mr Trotman can claim considerable success, but there is a suspicion that Ford 2000 may be a solution to yesterday's problems rather than a great leap forward. As one leading analyst observed:

'All Ford 2000 is aimed at doing is solving a problem that they had created.'

The Economist

G R A M M A R   R E V I E W

MANAGEMENT PLANS

1 Look at this conversation and underline the four verbs in the future tense.

> MANAGER   OK. This is the plan. We're going to launch our new product at the beginning of the year. And we're going to start the advertising campaign in early December.
>
> SALESMAN   Sorry, John. When are we going to tell our main customers about this?
>
> MANAGER   Good question. I'll deal with that in a minute.

2 Two different future tenses are used above. Explain why.

CHECK

You can use both *will* (or *'ll*) and *going to* to talk about a future intention.

Use *will* when you make your decision at the moment of speaking.

I'll deal with that later.

Use *going to* when you have taken your decision in advance.

We're going to launch our new product at the beginning of the year.

For more on the future tenses, turn to page 133

A STAFF MEETING

1 Listen to some workers asking questions about a new management policy. They ask about these four issues. Put a tick next to the issues on which the manager has already made a decision and a cross next to the ones that he hasn't.

redundancies	
a new bonus scheme	
health and safety	
shorter hours	

2 Compare your answers.

3 Listen again and notice the future form that the manager uses in each answer.

PRACTICE 1

Take turns to ask and answer these questions. When you answer, use *going to* if you have already taken a decision and *will* or *won't* if you haven't decided.

1 What are you going to do this weekend?

2 Where are you going to go on your next business trip?

3 What is your next car going to be?

4 Are you going to work late any night this week?

Now ask a few more questions about each other's intentions.

Talking about the future

THE FUTURE OF BUSINESS

We can also use *will* or *won't* to talk about predictions. Here are some predictions by Professor John Kay of the London Business School about the future of business.

1 Complete the text with *will* or *won't*.

> In the future, there (1)__*won't*__ be so many differences between the countries of the world and so companies (2)_____ become even more international. New technology (3)_____ create new opportunities. Personal space travel (4)_____ be possible and a space tourism industry (5)_____ develop. Meanwhile life (6)_____ be so easy for some of today's top companies. For example, the oil industry and car manufacturing (7)_____ almost certainly become less important. But some things (8)_____ change. Children (9)_____ have the same tastes and so companies like Coca-Cola and Disney (10)_____ continue to be successful.

2 🗣 Discuss which predictions you agree with.

PRACTICE 2

Draw a line that represents your idea of the ups and downs of the past, present and future of your career. Put a cross to show where you are at the moment. It could look like this.

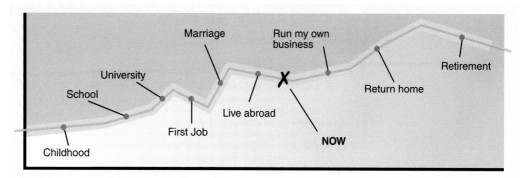

🗣 Show your line graph to your partner and ask and answer questions about the future. Ask questions like:

What are you going to do next year?
What do you think you'll do after you retire? etc.

PRACTICE 3

🗣 Try the following activities.

▌ **A** Explain briefly your view of the situation of your company in five years' time.
B Ask at least three questions.

▌ Swap roles.

doing **business** *Getting information*

THE FIRM In the film *The Firm*, Tom Cruise plays the part of Mitch McDeere, a brilliant young lawyer with several job offers from America's leading law firms. At the end of a job interview with the partners (senior lawyers) of the law firm Bendini, Lambert & Locke, they give him a sealed envelope.

Read the scene below and answer these questions:

1 In the room, which of the characters is the boss?
2 The four men are pretending to be in a particular situation. What is it?
3 What is the salary offer?

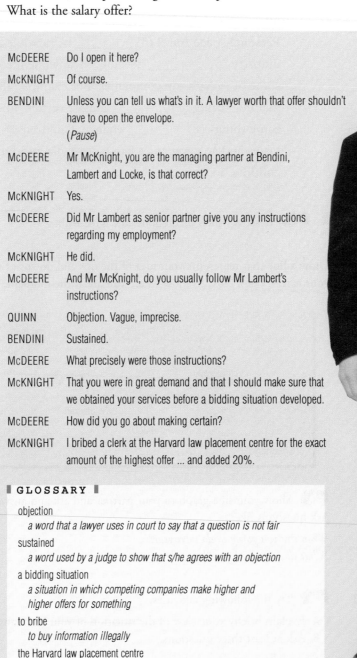

McDEERE	Do I open it here?
McKNIGHT	Of course.
BENDINI	Unless you can tell us what's in it. A lawyer worth that offer shouldn't have to open the envelope. (*Pause*)
McDEERE	Mr McKnight, you are the managing partner at Bendini, Lambert and Locke, is that correct?
McKNIGHT	Yes.
McDEERE	Did Mr Lambert as senior partner give you any instructions regarding my employment?
McKNIGHT	He did.
McDEERE	And Mr McKnight, do you usually follow Mr Lambert's instructions?
QUINN	Objection. Vague, imprecise.
BENDINI	Sustained.
McDEERE	What precisely were those instructions?
McKNIGHT	That you were in great demand and that I should make sure that we obtained your services before a bidding situation developed.
McDEERE	How did you go about making certain?
McKNIGHT	I bribed a clerk at the Harvard law placement centre for the exact amount of the highest offer ... and added 20%.

▌ **GLOSSARY** ▌

objection
a word that a lawyer uses in court to say that a question is not fair
sustained
a word used by a judge to show that s/he agrees with an objection
a bidding situation
a situation in which competing companies make higher and higher offers for something
to bribe
to buy information illegally
the Harvard law placement centre
an office at Harvard University that helps young lawyers to find jobs

OPEN AND CLOSED QUESTIONS

Closed questions ask for specific information. You can often answer with one piece of information or with *Yes/No*.

Open questions give people the chance to talk more freely. They often begin with *What, Why,* or *How*.

Look again at the film script and decide which of McDeere's questions are open and which are closed.

MEET THE STAFF

Leora, a new manager, is preparing for a series of individual meetings with the members of her new department. She wants to hear their opinions of recent changes in the company. Before the meetings, she makes a note of five things that she particularly wants to find out about.

1 Write the five questions that you would use to find out someone else's opinion on these five subjects. (They could be open or closed questions.)

> new arrangements in the office
> new management structure
> morale in the department
> training needs
> the department's progress over the past year

2 Compare your questions. Which are open and which are closed?

3 *1* Compare your questions to the manager's questions that you hear.

2 Could the manager have been more effective in the meeting? How?

QUESTIONING ROLES

Try the following activities.

▌ **A** Think of a product that you use every day, but don't tell **B** what it is.
  B Try to find out what product **A** has thought of, but do not ask directly what the product is.

▌ **B** Think of a job, but don't tell **A** what it is.
  A Try to find out what job **B** has thought of without asking directly.

2 doing business *An interview*

A JOB ADVERT   Read this job advertisement and answer these questions.

1 What kind of company is advertising?
2 Where is the job based?
3 What special skills are required?

AFRICA General manager

A large international energy company is looking for a general manager to run its east African office. Based in Nairobi, you will work closely with technical and operational specialists and play a leading role in all the company's commercial activities in the region.

You should be a graduate with a working knowledge of English. You must also have excellent communicative and interpersonal skills.

In addition to a performance-related salary, we provide an attractive benefits package.

Please reply with c.v. to:
Nicholl Executive Search, PO Box 1997, London, UK

NICHOLL EXECUTIVE SEARCH

THREE CANDIDATES   In small groups, discuss which of these people you think would be the best candidate for the job. Give your reasons.

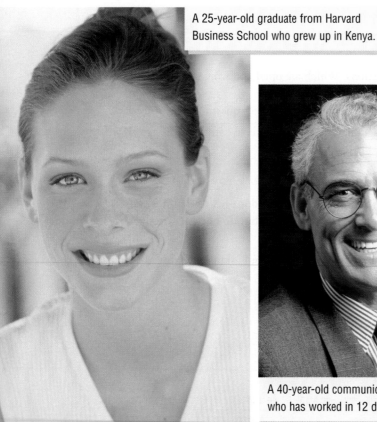

A 25-year-old graduate from Harvard Business School who grew up in Kenya.

A 40-year-old communications consultant who has worked in 12 different countries.

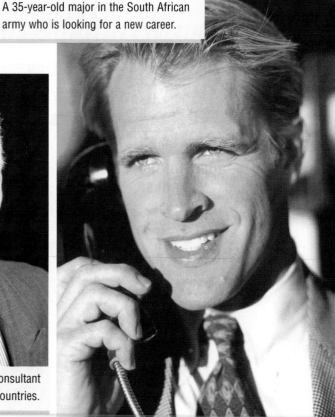

A 35-year-old major in the South African army who is looking for a new career.

PREPARING FOR AN INTERVIEW

To make its decision on the best person for the job, the company needs to find out about these four areas:

- the skills the candidates have
- their experience
- their personality
- their expectations

1 In groups, think of two or three questions to ask about each area.

2 Now look at the questions below. Which of the four areas is each of the questions asking about?

1 Do you think that you're a natural communicator?
2 What did you like most about your last job?
3 How do you try to motivate the people that you manage?
4 How do you spend your free time?
5 What kind of job would you like to have in five years' time?
6 Why did you leave your last job?
7 What do you think are your weak points?
8 How much do you expect to earn?

INTERVIEWING THE MAJOR

Now you will hear an interview with one of the candidates for the job.

1 Listen and then give the candidate marks out of ten in each of the four areas.

Skills   _____

Experience   _____

Personality _____

Expectations _____

2 Compare your marks with those of others in the group and discuss the differences. Would you give him the job?

INTERVIEWING ROLES

- A You are a senior manager who has recently joined B's company. You want to get to know B, so you invite B into your office to discuss a few personal and job-related questions.
  B Play yourself.
- B You are a journalist who is interviewing A for a magazine.
  A Play yourself.
- A You are applying for the job below.
  B Interview A.

■ **SALESPEOPLE FOR YOUNG BIOTECH CO.** ■

We are a biotechnology company based in Boston, Mass. and we are looking for new salespeople. You don't have to have specialist knowledge or years of experience. But you do need confidence, ambition and unlimited potential.

Do you have excellent communication skills? Do you have the right image for this young, thrusting organisation?

Then you could be the person for us!

Call 0101020 for an interview – right now!

focus

Management culture

THE DANCING BANK MANAGER

The photo above shows a manager from the UK's Lloyds Bank getting a ballet lesson as part of his management development. What lessons can managers learn from ballerinas?

THE X-Y TEST

1 Look at these pairs of statements. In each case, decide which statement you agree with.

1 a People are lazy and don't like work.
b People have a psychological need to work.
2 a People need control and the threat of punishment in order to work effectively.
b People want to achieve objectives.
3 a Most people avoid responsibility.
b Under the right conditions, most people want responsibility.

2 Work in small groups and give examples from your own experience to support your choices.

THEORY X AND THEORY Y

The management thinker, Douglas McGregor, used the terms Theory X and Theory Y to define two different management cultures. If you chose two or more 'a's in the section above, you probably agree with Theory X. If you chose two or more 'b's, you agree with Theory Y.

Here are definitions of Theory X and Theory Y. Which definition applies to which theory?

Theory? _____ *was based on traditional carrot and stick thinking. It said that work was a necessary evil to provide money.*

More optimistically, Theory? _____ *argued that people wanted and needed work.*

THEORY AND PRACTICE

Read these two descriptions of young people's experiences of American companies. In small groups, discuss which of the two theories best explains the management cultures in each.

1 Michael Lewis was a bond salesman for the American investment bank, Salomon Brothers, in the 1980s. Here he describes some advice he was given on his first training course.

LEARNING
to love your corporate culture

The man was telling us how to survive. 'You've got to think of Salomon Brothers as like a jungle ... and the guy you end up working for is your jungle leader. Whether you succeed here or not depends on knowing how to survive in the jungle. You've got to learn from your boss. He's key.' ♥

2 Here one of America's top businessmen, Stanley Bing, describes a job interview with an enthusiastic young man.

BOOGA-BOOGA!

BOOGA-BOOGA!

'I'm looking for an entry-level position in corporate relations. Maybe corporate marketing, if I get lucky,' he says.
'Really?' I say. 'Out of the entire realm of human possibility, that's what you want to do?' I'm sorry. What twenty-four-year-old really and truly wants to be in corporate marketing, for God's sake? The guy makes me want to stand up on my desk and yell, 'Booga-booga!' Instead, I say, 'Didn't you ever want to be a rock musician or a forest ranger or anything?'
There is no poetry in this dude. No soul. He makes me sad. I kick him out of my office.

GLOSSARY

realm *area*
dude *American slang for 'man'*

X, Y AND YOU

Work in small groups.

1 Do you think that your company works according to Theory X or Theory Y? Explain your reasons.
2 Which of the two theories is most effective for motivating people in your industry? Again, explain your reasons.

Developing a conversation

SOME CULTURAL DIFFERENCES

In *Riding the Waves of Culture*, his book on cultural diversity in business, the Dutch writer, Fons Trompenaars, shows how conversations develop in three different cultures. A and B are two people who are having a conversation. The black line shows when each one speaks, the spaces show when they are silent.

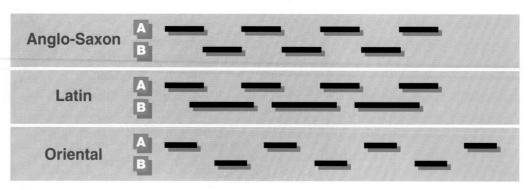

1 What does the diagram tell you about conversations in different cultures? Decide which of these sentences are true and which are false.

1 When speaking English, it is a good idea to leave long pauses.
2 People in Latin cultures often interrupt each other.
3 There are often short silences during conversations in Oriental cultures.
4 In Anglo-Saxon cultures, people often interrupt each other.

2 Compare these ideas to your experience of conversations with people from the three cultures.

REALLY?

Here are five sentences that a friend might use to start a conversation with you.

1 Have you heard that the price of phone calls is going to fall dramatically?

2 Someone told me that we're all going to do our shopping by computer within a few years.

3 Apparently, an American company is taking bookings for holidays in space.

4 Did you know that scientists are developing ways of building skyscrapers out of diamonds?

5 I heard that Ferrari are bringing out a new sports car next year.

social skills

1 How would you respond to each of the five sentences? Choose from:

| disbelief | interest | surprise | lack of interest | enthusiasm |

2 🔲 Listen to the way the woman responds to each sentence.

1 Which sentence doesn't she believe?
2 Which sentence does she find surprising?
3 What are her reactions to the other sentences?

REALLY ROLES

▌ **A** Say one of the sentences in the speech bubbles opposite.
  B Say 'Really?' to express one of the five emotions already mentioned.
  A Guess which emotion **B** is expressing.

▌ Swap roles.

THAT'S INTERESTING   🔲 Listen to the next part of the recording. This time the woman says more than 'Really'. Write down her responses and decide which of the five emotions above she is expressing.

RESPONSE	EMOTION

FINDING OUT MORE Here are two ways of developing a conversation further.

PROBING

You can use these phrases to ask for more information:

So, what are you saying?
What do you mean?
Tell me more.

RESTATING

You can also repeat a part of what the other person has just said. For example:

MAN   Have you heard that the price of phone calls is going to fall dramatically?

WOMAN   Dramatically?

MAN   Yes, you see ...

🔲 Listen to the next conversation and, as you listen, answer these questions:

1 What information does the woman get by probing?
2 What information does she get by restating?
3 When does she lose interest?
4 How does she end the conversation?

SOME INTERESTING ROLES

▌ **A** Tell **B** an interesting fact.
  B Find out more by probing and restating.

▌ Swap roles.

6 the **customer**

Sales VOCABULARY

NINE QUALITIES   Here are nine things that you may need to be when dealing with customers. Which do you think are the most important? Rank them from 1 to 9.

precise persuasive **polite**
positive practical
punctual persistent
prepared **patient**

WHAT THEY DON'T TEACH YOU   Mark McCormack is probably the most successful sports agent in the world. He represents the interests of hundreds of top sports stars. In his best-selling book, *What They Don't Teach You At The Harvard Business School*, he tells this story about dealing with a customer.

  Which of the above nine qualities does he show? Explain why.

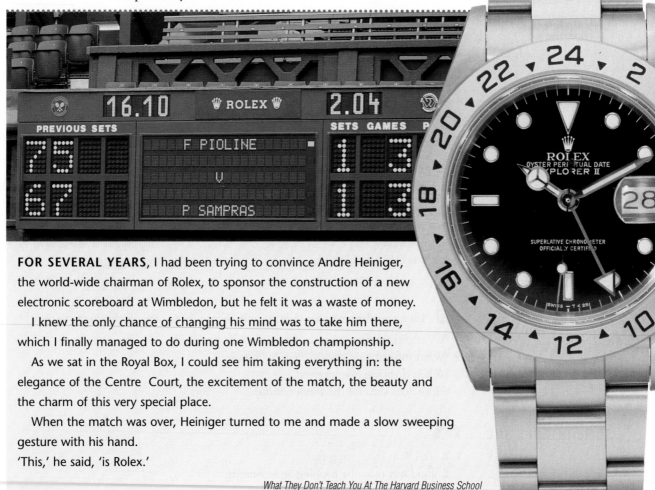

FOR SEVERAL YEARS, I had been trying to convince Andre Heiniger, the world-wide chairman of Rolex, to sponsor the construction of a new electronic scoreboard at Wimbledon, but he felt it was a waste of money.

I knew the only chance of changing his mind was to take him there, which I finally managed to do during one Wimbledon championship.

As we sat in the Royal Box, I could see him taking everything in: the elegance of the Centre Court, the excitement of the match, the beauty and the charm of this very special place.

When the match was over, Heiniger turned to me and made a slow sweeping gesture with his hand.

'This,' he said, 'is Rolex.'

What They Don't Teach You At The Harvard Business School

SPONSORSHIP

1 Mark McCormack talks about four of Wimbledon's special qualities. What are they? Write them in the box below.

WIMBLEDON	A PAVAROTTI CONCERT	THE WORLD CUP FINAL	A BOLSHOI BALLET	THE OSCAR CEREMONY

2 Now think of at least two words that you associate with the other four events.

3 What kind of company do you think is the best sponsor for each of these events? Give your reasons.

4 What kind of event do you think that your company should sponsor? Again, give your reasons.

FROM COMPANY TO CUSTOMER ...

Here are four activities that connect a business to its customers.

1 Match the number of the appropriate definition to each verb.

1 to give goods to someone else in exchange for money
2 to make something known to the public, for example in a newspaper or on television
3 to supply goods in a particular area
4 to pay for a show, broadcast, sports event, etc. in return for advertising

2 Work in groups and make as many words as you can from each verb and write them in the form of a network, like the example.

3 Ask and answer questions about the way your companies handle these six activities. (e.g. Do you do a lot of advertising? How do you distribute your products? How many salespeople do you have?)

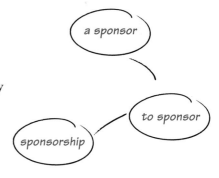

McCORMACK AND YOU

In his book, Mark McCormack also makes these statements about dealing with customers.

'I can't imagine anyone being effective in business without having some insight into people.'

'All things being equal, people will buy from a friend.'

'Effective selling is directly tied to timing, patience and persistence.'

'Just as there is a right time to make a sale, there is a right place for it as well.'

1 Read them and then look again at his story about Andre Heiniger and Wimbledon. Which of these ideas does the story illustrate?

2 Do you agree with Mark McCormack's four statements? Give examples from your own experience to justify your opinions.

G R A M M A R   R E V I E W

A LOAN ADVISER [cassette] You will hear a loan adviser at a bank discussing the arrangements for a loan with a customer. As you listen, fill in the details on this form.

LOAN APPLICATION DETAILS

Amount of loan   £ _____

Period of loan   _____

Total amount repayable   £ _____

Monthly repayments   £ _____

Loan protection scheme?   YES / NO

FIRST OR SECOND CONDITIONAL? Here are two sentences from the conversation on the tape.

> If you want to borrow for longer, it'll be slightly more.

> What would happen if you lost your job?

1 Notice that different forms of the verb are used in the two sentences. Discuss why this is.

2 Listen again to the recording and fill in the gaps using the correct form of the verbs that are used.

1 If I _____ (borrow) £3000, how much _____ (I pay back)?

2 If you _____ (take) a three-year option, that _____ (be) £106 per month.

3 If you _____ (die), _____ (your family be able to) pay back this loan?

4 So if anything _____ (happen) to you, you _____ (not have to) worry about repayments.

3 Why are different forms of the verb used in these sentences?

█ CHECK

Here is a way of remembering the use of first and second conditional sentences in English.

First conditional

REALISTIC CONDITION → RESULT	
If you *do* that,	this *will happen*.
present simple	*'will' future*

Second conditional

HYPOTHETICAL CONDITION → RESULT	
If you *did* that,	this *would happen*.
past simple	*'would' + verb*

█ *For more on first and second conditional sentences, turn to page 130* █

Conditionals

PRACTICE

1 Put the verbs into the correct forms.

1 What _____ (you do) if it _____ (rain) this weekend?

2 What _____ (you do) if another company _____ (offer) you a job with a much bigger salary?

3 What _____ (you do) if your boss _____ (ask) you to work late tomorrow?

4 What _____ (you do) if you _____ (find) a burglar in your house after work this evening?

5 What _____ (happen) to your company if the price of oil _____ (double)?

2 👥 Which of the above are realistic and which are hypothetical speculations?

ELISION

When *will* or *would* are used to make questions, they are normally pronounced in full. However, in other situations, some sounds from these words can be left out – or 'elided'.
For example:

> will ➔ 'll, will not ➔ won't, would ➔ 'd, would not ➔ wouldn't

1 👥 Take turns to *answer* the five questions in *Practice* above, eliding the words when appropriate.

2 📼 Check your answers.

A MARKET DILEMMA

1 At the moment, company A and company B both have a good position in the market. But both companies are worried that the other one will decide to cut its prices. This matrix sums up the position. Study it and complete these sentences.

1 If company A cuts prices and company B doesn't, _____

2 If company B cuts prices and company A doesn't, _____

3 If neither company cuts prices, _____

4 If both companies cut prices, _____

2 👥 Discuss what you would do if you were one of the companies in this situation. Give your reasons.

		Company A	
		Keep prices the same	Cut prices
Company B	Keep prices the same	Profits stay the same	A: Profits rise by 20% B: Profits fall by 30%
	Cut prices	A: Profits fall by 30% B: Profits rise by 20%	Profits fall by 30%

doing **business** *Bargaining*

WHY NEGOTIATE? In small groups, discuss which of these statements you most agree with. Explain why.

▮ In any negotiation, you should always try to get the most for yourself.

▮ A negotiation is an opportunity to create a long-term business relationship.

▮ A negotiation should bring benefits to both sides.

HANDLING A DIFFICULT CUSTOMER Patrick Ellis is an international expert on sales. Here are some of his ideas on handling a difficult situation with a customer.

1 Read the text and then, in small groups, discuss these points.

1 Which of the three approaches do you think would be most effective? Give your reasons.

2 Can you think of any other ways of dealing with the situation? Decide what you would say to this customer.

SITUATION

You are selling a product for £1800, but your customer only wants to pay £1500.
Here are three things that you could say to the customer.

'If I were in your position, I would also want to get the best possible price. But we're both in business to make a profit and we're only talking about a £300 difference. If you meet me half way, I'll work out a nice little deal for you. What do you say?'

'This is crazy. If we were criminals, we would try to help each other. But we're not. We're honest businesspeople and we can't reach an agreement. Now I want to help you, so this is what I'll do. I'm going to take a coin out of my pocket and toss it. You can call "Heads" or "Tails". If you call correctly, I'll give you the product for £1750. But if you call incorrectly, you'll pay me the full price. How does that sound to you?'

'If you make me a reasonable offer, say £1750, then we can shake hands. If I accepted anything less, I wouldn't make a profit. If you don't want to pay that much for it then, I'm sorry, but I won't sell it to you.'

---

2 Look again at the three solutions offered by Patrick Ellis and underline the eight conditional sentences that are used.

3 Which of these sentences describe hypothetical situations? Decide why these situations are hypothetical.

A PHOTOCOPIER SALESMAN

📼 You'll hear a photocopier salesman Mr Belew, bargaining with a customer, Mr Jones.

1 Listen and make a note of who says each of these sentences, then fill in the blank spaces with the correct forms of the verbs.

1 If you _____ (buy) this copier from me today, I _____ (give) you a two-year guarantee and 15% off the normal purchase price.

2 If I _____ (buy) a new photocopier now, my bank manager _____ (go) crazy.

3 What _____ (you say) if I offered you six months' interest-free credit?

4 If you _____ (give) me a two-year guarantee, 15% off and six months' interest-free credit, I _____ (take) one.

2 👥 For each sentence, decide why different conditional forms are used.

SALES ROLES

👥

A You want to buy a car. Its price is £9,000 but you only want to pay £8,000.
B You are a secondhand car salesman.

Look at these instructions, work out what you will say and then have the conversation.

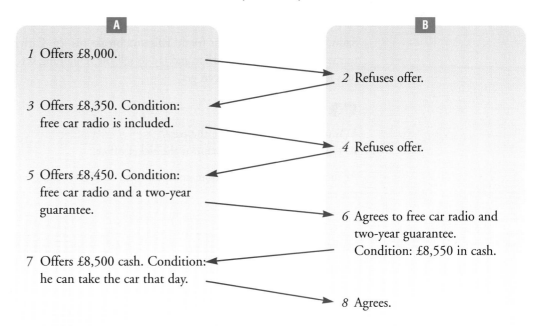

2 doing **business** *Negotiating roles*

TWO FOOLS?

'There are two fools in any market; one asks too little, one asks too much.'

Russian proverb

In small groups, talk about these questions:

1 Why is it stupid to ask too much for a product?
And – why is it stupid to ask too little?

2 Does this proverb tell you anything about good negotiating?

THE SKI PASS NEGOTIATION

You are on holiday with a friend at a ski resort in Colorado, USA. A lift pass at this resort costs $25 a day, but to avoid the long daily queues at the ticket office, you both decide to buy a ten-day ski pass for $200 at the beginning of your holiday.

Sadly, on the third day, your friend falls and breaks his leg. Early next morning, you go to the queue at the ticket office and try to sell the remaining seven days of your friend's pass for the best price you can get.

A You are the person selling the pass.
B You are waiting in the queue at the ticket office.

At the end of your negotiation, compare your results with those of others in the class.

THE ANTIQUE STALL
NEGOTIATION

A You want to buy a few things from this antique stall. Although the prices are clearly displayed, you think you can get a better deal.

B You are the owner of this antique stall.

Before starting the negotiation, **A** should turn to page 125 and **B** should turn to page 126.

At the end of your negotiations, compare what was bought and what was spent with other pairs in the class.

focus

Four negotiating problems

Gavin Kennedy runs a consultancy firm specialising in negotiating and has written several books on the subject. In his book, *Everything Is Negotiable*, he asks his readers to solve a number of negotiating problems. Here are four of them.

WHAT'S YOUR BEST PRICE?

1 🗣️ Read this problem and make a list of pros and cons for each of the four possible solutions. Choose the solution which you think is best.

You are a manufacturer of engine parts. After many cancellations, you have been given an interview with the boss of Europe's largest car firm. But he insists that you meet him at the airport a few minutes before he flies to Australia. This is your big chance! While walking towards passport control, he opens with a demand for your best price for a six-month contract to supply parts. What do you do?

☞ **a)** Give him your lowest price immediately.

☞ **b)** Start slightly higher than your lowest price.

☞ **c)** Start with a high price to give yourself room to negotiate.

☞ **d)** Say 'Have a nice flight!'

2 🗣️ Find a different partner and have the conversation between you and the car firm's boss.

3 Compare your ideas with Gavin Kennedy's solution to this problem on page 125.

GOING ROUND IN CIRCLES

🗣️ Read this problem and discuss what each solution communicates to the Japanese producer. Choose the solution which you think is best and then read Gavin Kennedy's thoughts on page 125.

You are in Tokyo negotiating for a long-term contract with a Japanese producer and the negotiations have been stuck for several days. It feels like you are going round in circles. What do you do?

☞ **a)** Wait for them to make the first move?

☞ **b)** Make a small concession.

☞ **c)** Change the subject entirely.

☞ **d)** Take a break.

DAMAGED GOODS

1  Choose your solution to this problem and then have the conversation between you and the manager of the bookshop.

> You are in a bookshop, looking for a book to read on holiday. There are several copies of the book you want but one of them is slightly damaged. What do you do?
>
> ☞ **a)** Select a a non-damaged copy.
> ☞ **b)** Take the damaged copy to the desk.
> ☞ **c)** Take the damaged copy and the non-damaged copy to the desk.

2 Discuss which solution gets the best result.

3 Again compare your ideas with those on page 125.

A SHARPLY-DRESSED MAN

1 Choose your solution to this problem and give your reasons.

> You're negotiating with a man who's wearing a beautiful Savile Row suit, a gold Rolex watch and Gucci shoes. How do you rate his status?
>
> ☞ **a)** low
> ☞ **b)** high
> ☞ **c)** difficult to decide

2 Discuss what kind of clothes you would wear to an important negotiation. Give your reasons.

Gavin Kennedy's ideas are on page 125.

FOLLOW-UP When you've discussed all the problems and have read Gavin Kennedy's suggestions, talk about these points:

▌ Do you agree with Kennedy's solutions to all the problems? Give your reasons.
▌ What lessons about good negotiating is he trying to teach?

Restaurants

MENUS It is often difficult to translate menus from one language into another. In this menu, there is at least one mistake in every line!

1 Find as many mistakes as you can. (It will probably help to use a dictionary.)

RESTAURANT MENU

Arthur Grubby's

BEGINNERS
Asparagus soap
Stuffed fungus
Mixed things

FEATHERED DISHES
Chicken's chest with tomatoes and cheese
Little duck with the orange
Roast peasant (hung)

FLESH
Part of cow in cognac (enflamed by chef at the table)
Slice of pig (heated)
Boiled sheep pieces with root vegetables

SEA FRUIT
Just dead lobster
Grilled leg of salmon in sauce
Peeled trout and nuts

BUDDINGS
Ice cream (imposed from the USA!)
A selection of fruit from the car

All our main dishes are equipped with choice of salad or
a selection of plucked vegetables

2 Compare your findings with those of other people in the group. Can you guess what the items should be?

3 Which dishes on the menu do you still not understand? Think of questions that you could ask a waiter to find out more about them.

4 Compare your ideas with the correct version of the menu on page 125.

social skills

A FEW QUESTIONS ABOUT THE MENU

1 🔲 You'll hear two people talking to a waiter about the menu opposite. Listen and answer these questions.

1 Which three items do they ask him about? Fill the gaps in these questions.

What do you mean by _____ ?

How exactly is the _____ cooked?

And what's a _____ ?

2 What does the waiter recommend?

2 🔲 Now listen again and answer these questions.

1 What is the first item they discuss normally called?

2 How is the second item cooked?

3 What's wrong with the third item?

PAYING

Read the story below about the end of a business dinner in a restaurant.

1 From this list, choose the most appropriate phrase for each step in the story.

a Can I have a receipt, please?

b OK. This is on me.

c Do you accept credit cards?

d No, really, I insist.

e Can I have the bill, please?

f Is service included?

THE STORY	THE PHRASE
1 At the end of the meal, he said that he would pay for everyone.	
2 We said that he shouldn't pay for us all, but he didn't want to listen.	
3 So, he asked the waiter for the bill.	
4 When it arrived, it wasn't clear whether he should tip or not.	
5 He looked in his wallet and found that he didn't have enough cash.	
6 But, of course, he wasn't worried because his company was paying for everything.	

2 👥 Can you think of other phrases that you can use in each of the above situations?

7 production

Production VOCABULARY

EFFICIENT PRODUCTION

1 What makes an efficient production process? Here are seven things which could be important. Rank them from 1 to 7.

- large inventories* of parts
- plenty of space
- good communication
- strict quality control

- fair division of labour amongst workers
- smooth flow of production through the factory
- good safety procedures

GLOSSARY

inventories (US)
stocks (UK)

2 What other factors do you think are important in an efficient production process?

THE MACHINE THAT CHANGED THE WORLD

The Machine That Changed The World is a book that contains the results of a $5 million research project which examined the reasons for the success of Japanese car manufacturers.

Below is its description of two car factories: a General Motors plant at Framingham in the USA and a Toyota plant at Takaoka in Japan.

1 Read the text and make notes like those in the table on the opposite page, listing the differences between the Toyota and GM factories.

THE DIFFERENCES between Takaoka and Framingham are striking to anyone who understands the logic of lean production.

Toyota's philosophy about the amount of plant space is just the opposite of GM's at Framingham: Toyota believes there should be as little space as possible, This means that face-to-face communication among workers is easier, and there is little room to store inventories. GM, by contrast, believes that extra space is necessary so that people can work on vehicles which need repairs. They can also store the large inventories required for smooth production.

The final assembly line revealed further differences. Less than an hour's worth of inventory was next to each worker at Takaoka. The parts went on more smoothly and the worker tasks were better balanced, so that every worker worked at about the same pace. When a worker found a defective part, he sent it to the quality control area in order to obtain a replacement ...

At Takaoka, each worker can pull a cord just above the work station to stop the line if any problem is found; at GM only senior managers can stop the line for any reason other than safety – although it stops frequently ... At Takaoka the line is almost never stopped.

At the end of the line the difference between lean and mass production was even more striking. At Takaoka, we observed almost no rework area at all. Almost every car was driven directly from the line to the boat or trucks taking cars to the buyer.

The Machine That Changed The World by Womack, Jones and Roos

GENERAL MOTORS	TOYOTA
lots of extra space	*as little space as possible*
room to do repairs	*easy face-to-face communication*

2 🗣 Discuss your lists.

A FEW DEFINITIONS

1 🗣 Explain the meanings of these expressions that you met in the text.

- ▌ assembly line   ▌ defective   ▌ lean production
- ▌ work station   ▌ rework area

2 Check your answers in a dictionary.

GM v. TOYOTA

🗣 Look again at your lists and make at least five sentences comparing GM with Toyota.

You can use the words *whereas* or *while* to make a comparison,

e.g.   GM believes there should be plenty of plant space *whereas/while* Toyota believes there should be as little space as possible.

or use comparative adjectives,

e.g.   There is *more* plant space at GM.
Face-to-face communication is *easier* at Toyota.

PRODUCTION AND YOU

Now work in small groups and compare your company's production process to the system used by Toyota. (If you don't work for a manufacturing company, talk about any production process that you know e.g. making wine, pottery or even a wooden table!)

What lessons could your company learn from Toyota?

G R A M M A R   R E V I E W

FACTORY CONDITIONS

1  Which of these sentences do you agree or disagree with?

■ Workers are more productive when music is being played in a factory.

■ Output is improved when conditions are made more comfortable for workers.

■ Less management time is wasted when managers spend more time talking face-to-face with factory workers.

■ Breaks should be taken at regular intervals, but production should not be interrupted at any other time.

2 Underline the verbs in the sentences above which are in the passive form.

THE HAWTHORNE EXPERIMENTS

In the Hawthorne Experiments, researchers tried to find out how working conditions affected productivity.

1 🔲 Listen to the description of the Hawthorne Experiments and complete this summary by putting the verbs in brackets into the correct passive form.

The Hawthorne Experiments

A SUMMARY

The Hawthorne experiments (1) .... (conduct) by Elton Mayo in Chicago in the 1920s. More than 20,000 workers at Western Electric's Hawthorne Plant (2) .... (involve).

In the first experiment, lighting conditions in the Hawthorne factory (3) .... (improve); in this case, it (4) .... (find) that output also improved. In the second experiment, lighting conditions (5) .... (make) worse. Unexpectedly, output went up again. Finally, lighting conditions in the factory (6) .... (return) to normal. Much to Mayo's surprise, once again, the workers' productivity improved.

2 🔲 Check your summary by listening again.

THE HAWTHORNE EFFECT

1 Work in small groups. Discuss the explanation for the increases in productivity in the Hawthorne Experiments.

2 🔲 Compare your ideas with Elton Mayo's interpretation of his experiments.

Describing processes

CHECK

The passive of a verb is formed by using *to be* in the appropriate tense and adding the past participle of the verb.

For example:

Active	Passive
He is doing it.	*It is being done (by him).*
He will do it.	*It will be done (by him).*
He did it.	*It was done (by him).*

▎ *For more on passives, see page 137* ▎

A HAMBURGER PRODUCTION PROCESS

This flow diagram is one way of showing a production process that might be used in a hamburger restaurant.

Take turns to describe each step in the process, using the passive form as appropriate.

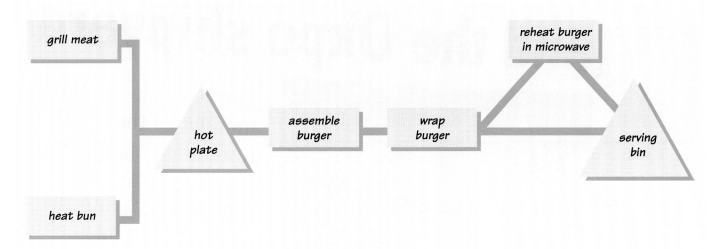

grill meat

heat bun

hot plate

assemble burger

wrap burger

reheat burger in microwave

serving bin

COMPARING PROCESSES

1 Listen to the way that burgers are produced at a fictional hamburger restaurant.

2 Work in small groups. List the differences between the process in the flow chart and the process described on the tape. (Remember to use the passive as appropriate.)

3 Compare your lists with others in the class.

PRACTICE 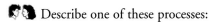 Describe one of these processes:

▎ making a pizza   ▎ changing the wheel of a car   ▎ building a brick wall.

doing business *Causes and effects*

DAEWOO

The South Korean company, Daewoo, was founded in 1967 and now employs more than 100,000 people. But its success hasn't always come easily. In fact, some parts of this giant corporation have had many ups and downs.

Take turns to describe this bar chart year by year.

THE OKPO SHIPYARD

Read the story behind the Daewoo bar chart and answer these questions.

1 What was the condition of the shipyard when Kim Woo Chong took it over?

2 Why was 1986 a bad year?

3 Why was 1993 a great year for the company?

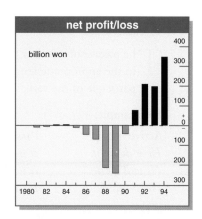

Daewoo
and the Okpo shipyard

OKPO SHIPYARD

Kim Woo Chong, the founder of the South Korean company, Daewoo, never really meant to get into the shipbuilding business.

In fact, he only took over the giant shipyard at Okpo in 1978 as a result of government pressure. 'I did not have a chance to say no,' he explains.

At the time, only 30% of the shipyard had been built and the company was nearly bankrupt. Its problems got worse the following year when South Korea's president, Park Chung Hee was assassinated – an event which led to serious political instability in the country. On top of that, a slump in shipping in the early 80s caused a sharp fall in the price of ships.

Things improved slightly in 1982 due to an order for 12 large ships from US Lines. To cope, the shipyard's workforce was increased dramatically. Then, in 1986, US Lines went bankrupt still owing Daewoo hundreds of millions of dollars. The company was again plunged into crisis.

In 1988, Daewoo's losses were still rising, when Mr Kim worked out a rescue package. Hundreds of millions of dollars were invested in the company and the production process was completely re-organised. By 1991, things were getting slightly better and in 1993 the company won orders for 54 ships worth $2.8 billion – the largest number of new orders for any shipyard in the world!

The Economist *26.11.94*

REASONS WHY

1 Look again at the text and match these causes and effects.

CAUSE	EFFECT
1 an order for 12 ships	*a* a fall in the price of ships
2 government pressure	*b* political instability
3 the president's assassination	*c* Daewoo's takeover of the Okpo shipyard
4 a slump in shipping	*d* the improvement in 1982

2 In the text, these four phrases link the above causes and effects together. Look at the text and decide which links a cause to an effect and which links an effect to a cause.

led to as a result of
due to caused

For example

CAUSE → EFFECT

'The assassination of the president *led to* political instability ...'

3 Use the links to complete these sentences.

1 The shipyard's workforce increased in the early 80s _____ the order for 12 ships.

2 The bankruptcy of US Lines _____ the company's crisis in 1986.

3 Mr Kim's investment and reorganisation _____ an improvement in 1991.

REASON ROLES

▌ Look at this graph of Daewoo's sales. Try to explain its ups and downs over the period.

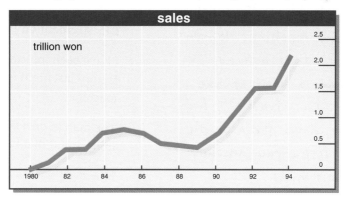

▌ Explain the ups and downs of your company (or a company you know well) over the past five years. Give reasons for what you describe.

doing **business** *Putting it in writing*

WRITE IT OR SAY IT?   In business, is it better to write something down or to say it on the phone or in a meeting? Here are three reasons why you might prefer to write something down on paper.

▮ You don't want to speak to the other person.
▮ The material needs to be kept for future reference.
▮ You need proof that you have taken action.

Work in small groups. What other reasons would you add to the list?

TWO REPORTS   Work in pairs and compare the accident report form and the memo. Talk about these questions.

1 What is the difference in the content of the two?
2 What is the difference in style?

ACCIDENT REPORT FORM

1/8/98

Dear Bob,
 I thought you should know that we've had a few problems on the night shift. I'm afraid that one of the lads has caught his arm in a machine. He went off to hospital — but it's nothing too serious. He's made a mess of the machine, though, I'm afraid. I had to shut the line down for a couple of hours, so we lost a fair amount of production last night.
 We followed all the procedures, so there's nothing to worry about but I'll talk you through it when I get back to work this evening.

 Alf

MEMORANDUM

Date   1.8.98

From   Bob Russell, **FACTORY MANAGER**

To   Cynthia Prytherch, **PRODUCTION CONTROLLER**

RE: Accident on production line

I have been informed that there was an accident at the factory last night involving a worker and one of our machines.

The man in question was taken to hospital, although I understand that he was not seriously hurt.

However, the machine was damaged and, as a result, the production line had to be shut down for two hours with a corresponding loss of production.

I have been assured that proper health and safety procedures were followed, but I am, of course, investigating the incident to see if any lessons can be learnt.

COMPARING STYLES   Look at these pairs of phrases from the two documents.

1 a I thought you should know ...

   b I have been informed that ...

2 a I had to shut the line down for a couple of hours.

   b The production line had to be shut down for two hours.

3 a We followed all the procedures, so there's nothing to worry about.

   b I have been assured that proper health and safety procedures were followed.

In each case, Bob Russell has used the passive rather than the active form of the verb. This moves the focus of the sentence from the subject to the object.

1   Why do you think Bob Russell has done this? Here are a few ideas:

▮ He wants to give an 'official' impression.

▮ He wants to make it less personal or more formal.

▮ He doesn't know who the subject of the sentence was. (Or at least he wants to give that impression!)

2 What other examples of differences in style can you find?

WRITING ROLE   **1** You are Angela's manager. How would you write to your manager to explain this situation?

Urgent Message

To _Mike_   From _Angela_

Date _10/8/98_   No. of pages _1_

Dear Mike,

I've done something terrible. You know the laptop computer? Well, I borrowed it from the office to do some work at home last night — and I left it on the train this morning. I called the railway company, but they say there's almost no chance of getting it back. What am I going to do?

Angela.

2 Compare your memo with those of others in the class.

focus

Building a team

A SUCCESSFUL TEAM In his book *Key Management Ideas*, the management writer Stuart Crainer lists these five roles which, he says, contribute to a successful team.

knower solver *doer* **checker** carer

1 Match the roles to these descriptions.

Who's who?

1 ROLE .... helps the team to solve problems by having ideas or finding resources from outside the team.	**CHARACTERIZED BY** innovation, imagination, good at socializing and negotiating
2 ROLE .... concentrates on the job. Gets it started, gets it done and makes sure that it's finished.	**CHARACTERIZED BY** high energy, good at motivating others, attention to detail
3 ROLE .... shows concern for the whole process and realism. Provides a balanced view of quality and time.	**CHARACTERIZED BY** good judgement, critical thinking, good use of individual talents
4 ROLE .... shows concern for individuals in the team and their progress.	**CHARACTERIZED BY** supportive and democratic approach, flexibility, concern for others
5 ROLE .... provides specialist knowledge or experience.	**CHARACTERIZED BY** dedication, high standards

2 Work in small groups. Which of these roles do you play in your job? Give at least two examples of things that you do, to support your answer.

BUILD YOUR OWN TEAM Imagine that you have to put together a management team to run a new global media business with interests in interactive TV, pop music and digital publishing. The team will be responsible for the group's strategy as well as the day-to-day running of the group.

1 Read the profiles of the seven international personalities opposite and discuss what else you know about them and their business style.

2 Think of two adjectives to sum up each of them.

3 Work in small groups and decide which five of these seven people most closely match the five roles above. Do you think that the five people you've chosen would really work together successfully as a team? Give your reasons.

4 Compare your ideas with the rest of the class.

With interests in property, retail and TV, Italian tycoon, Silvio Berlusconi, is one of Italy's top businesspeople. But he has also proved that his skills are not limited to the commercial world. Not only is he the boss of AC Milan, one of Europe's top football clubs, but, for a short period of time in 1994, he was even Italy's Prime Minister!

Silvio Berlusconi

Bill Gates

Bill Gates started in the computer industry when he was at school and was a billionaire by the age of 31. A combination of technical brilliance and fiercely competitive business tactics quickly made him the most powerful man in Silicon Valley – but he wanted his company Microsoft to be more than just a software house and in recent years it has diversified into many new fields.

Since her first hit in 1981, Madonna has proved that she is more than just an ordinary pop star. She has had considerable success in film, video and publishing, while her business skills have helped her to become one of the highest-paid women in the world. (In 1992 she earned $40 million.)

Madonna

Nikki Lauda

In the business world, the Austrian, Nikki Lauda, has shown the same courage, dedication and attention to detail that once made him the world's top Formula One racing driver. At his airline, Lauda Air, he is very much a 'hands-on' boss and even flies his own planes!

Akio Morita was one of the founders of Japan's giant Sony® corporation – and its boss for many years. He trained as an engineer and throughout his career he made sure that Sony® was at the leading edge of technology. He also had a brilliant understanding of the market and was responsible for the success of the Sony Walkman®.

Akio Morita

Anita Roddick

Since it started in 1976, Anita Roddick's Body Shop has grown from a one-woman business to become a multinational cosmetics company. Roddick is famous for not using advertising – instead she gets publicity through campaigns on international social and environmental issues.

Ted Turner launched the international TV news network CNN in 1980. Much of its success has been due to Turner's bold risk-taking and tough, inspirational management. He once told his employees, 'We're on a pirate ship at sea. We're going to go out and raid all the other ships on the ocean.'

Ted Turner

P R O F I L E S

Mixing business and pleasure

CULTURE AND LUNCH

Polly Platt is a consultant who specialises in helping people from different cultures to communicate. Read her description of a way of doing business and, in groups, discuss these questions.

'If you have some time, go to a current art exhibition, so you can discuss it over lunch, which is where 80% of the deals are made. It's important to realise that most of the conversation over lunch is not about business, it's about culture, politics, people in the news. Very often, the business at hand is only brought up at the end of lunch, or on the walk back to the office.'

1 Which of the following countries do you think is being described: USA, Germany, Italy, Japan, UK, France?

2 Explain why you think this is the case.

3 Would you give this advice to a visitor to your country? In what ways would your advice be different?

HIGH AND LOW CONTEXT

When discussing the relationship between business and pleasure, business thinkers talk about the two kinds of culture described below. Read the two descriptions and then discuss the questions underneath.

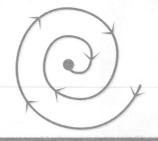

HIGH CONTEXT

People from high context cultures believe that you need to get to know the other person before you can do business with them. So you begin by discussing general points and then move on to the specific detail of the business deal.

From general to specific

LOW CONTEXT

In low context cultures, business comes first. You might discuss other things with your business partner, but only if there is enough time at the end of the meeting!

From specific to general

1 Which of the countries listed above do you think are high context and which do you think are low context?

2 How would you classify other countries that you have visited?

TOPICS OF CONVERSATION

When you go out for a business lunch or dinner, what do you expect to discuss? Here are a few ideas.

economics family *only business* **sport** politics **news** art *food* people you know *films*

TALKING ABOUT INTERESTS

1 Listen to the first extract from a conversation between two businesspeople in a restaurant and answer these questions.

1 Which of the topics of conversation in the box above is being discussed?

2 Which three phrases from the list below are used in the conversation?

   a How do you find that?
   b Did you watch the news this morning?
   c Have you seen the new Spielberg movie yet?
   d What did you like about it?
   e Are you interested in sport?
   f What do you do in your spare time?
   g What do you play?
   h What do you think?

2 Write the letters of the three phrases that are used in the appropriate place in this table.

INTRODUCTORY QUESTIONS	BEING MORE SPECIFIC	ASKING FOR AN OPINION

3 Listen to the next two extracts from the conversation and write the letters of the remaining sentences above in the appropriate places in the table.

SOME MORE INTERESTING ROLES

Have the following conversations. Try to use this pattern:

Introductory question → More specific question → An opinion

▌ **A** Ask **B** questions about how he or she spends their free time.
▌ **B** Ask **A** about a recent programme on TV.
▌ Develop short conversations on at least two other interests, following the same pattern.

8 business and society

Economic VOCABULARY

WHO SAID THAT?

On the opposite page are extracts from speeches made by these four national leaders.

Match the politicians to their speeches and discuss the reasons for your choices. Turn to page 126 for the answers.

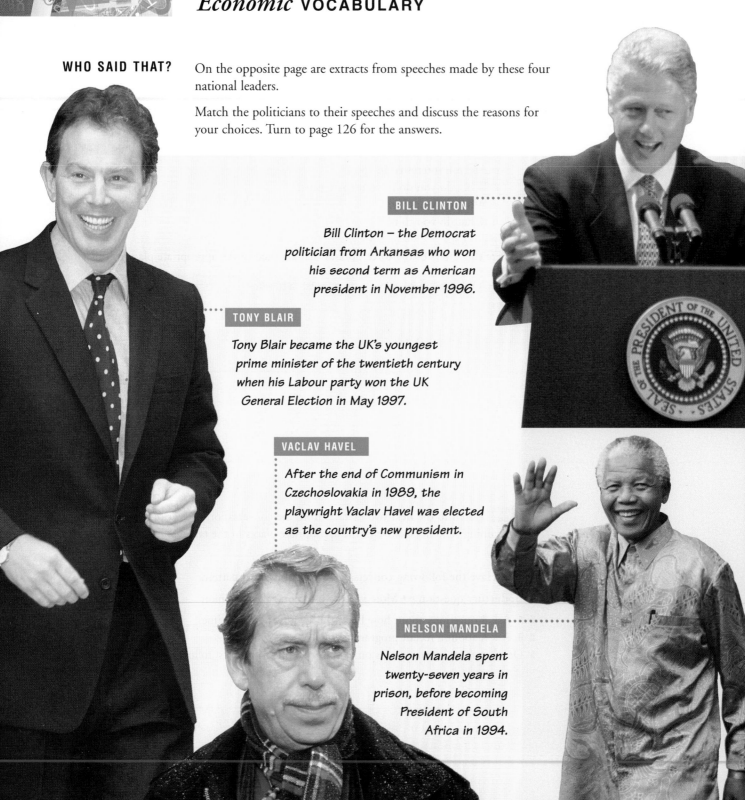

BILL CLINTON

Bill Clinton – the Democrat politician from Arkansas who won his second term as American president in November 1996.

TONY BLAIR

Tony Blair became the UK's youngest prime minister of the twentieth century when his Labour party won the UK General Election in May 1997.

VACLAV HAVEL

After the end of Communism in Czechoslovakia in 1989, the playwright Vaclav Havel was elected as the country's new president.

NELSON MANDELA

Nelson Mandela spent twenty-seven years in prison, before becoming President of South Africa in 1994.

1 'So tonight let us resolve to build that bridge to the 21st century ... Let us build a bridge ... to break the cycle of poverty and dependence, to protect our environment for generations to come and to maintain our world leadership for peace and freedom.'

2 'The apartheid destruction of our subcontinent is incalculable. The fabric of family life of millions of my people has been shattered. Millions are homeless and unemployed. Our economy lies in ruins and our people are embroiled in political strife.'

4 'I certainly believe that when there is no overriding reason for preferring the public provision of goods and services ... then the presumption should be that economic activity is best left to the private sector with market forces being fully encouraged to operate.'

3 'Our country is not flourishing. The enormous creative and spiritual potential of our nation is not being used sensibly. Entire branches of industry are producing goods which are of no interest to anyone, while we are lacking the things we need.'

GLOSSARY

embroiled	*involved*
strife	*troubles*
overriding	*most important*
presumption	*principle*

ECONOMIC PROBLEMS

Extracts 1–3 describe some problems associated with the economy.

social breakdown	
inflation	
unemployment	
poverty	
trade deficit	
inefficiency	
pollution	

1 Which of these problems are described in each of the three extracts? Put the appropriate number in the box.

2 Write three sentences which summarise the first three extracts.

3 Compare your sentences in small groups and talk about the differences between them.

PUBLIC AND PRIVATE SECTORS

Extract 4 talks about the public (state) and private (commercial) sectors of an economy.

1 Match the terms in the left-hand column with the appropriate descriptions in the right-hand column.

transport infrastructure	the army, navy and air force
utilities	payments for people who have retired from work
defence	help for people who are unemployed or very poor
pensions	the supply of gas, water, electricity
social security	road and railway networks, airports, etc.

2 In your country, which of the above areas are in the public sector and which are in the private sector?

3 In small groups, discuss how you think the speaker of extract 4 would divide the items in the list between the public and private sectors.

THE ECONOMY AND YOU

In small groups, discuss these points.

- What do you think is the biggest economic problem facing your country at the moment?
- In your ideal economy, how would you divide the above list between the public and private sectors? Add other areas that you think are interesting for your discussion (e.g. health, education, telecommunications).

G R A M M A R   R E V I E W

UK DEDUCTIONS   Here are some facts about the economy of the UK.

1 Match each fact with one of the deductions below.

◀ Nearly 50% of families with children have a computer; only around 20% of families without children have a computer.

GDP rose between 1981 and 1990, fell for the next two years and then rose again in 1993. ▶

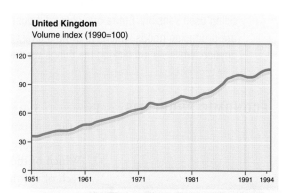

United Kingdom
Volume index (1990=100)

◀ Nearly 1 million people enter Central London every morning between 7 a.m. and 10 a.m.

The number of people in full-time education over the age of 16 has doubled since 1981. ▶

1 It can't be easy travelling into Central London in the morning.
2 A lot of parents must buy computers for their children.
3 There must have been economic problems in the early 90s.
4 There can't have been very many college and university students in the early 80s.

2 Look at the form of the verbs in the four sentences. How do you make a positive deduction and how do you make a negative one?

> ### CHECK
>
> When you're making a deduction in a positive sentence, use *must* before the main verb.
>
> *A lot of parents must buy computers for their children.*
>
> In negative sentences or questions, use *can't.*
>
> *It can't be easy travelling into Central London in the morning.*
>
> ❙ *For more on positive and negative deductions, see page 135* ❙

Analysing the facts

MORE UK FACTS

In the box are some more facts about the economy of the UK.

Complete these sentences to make four deductions.

1 People _____ be earning more today than in the past.

2 There _____ a very high demand for houses in Northern Ireland.

3 Industrial relations _____ improved since 1984.

4 There _____ been quite a lot of inflation over that period.

In 1971, the average household spent 20% of its income on food. In 1994, the figure was 11%.

In 1984, 27 million days' work were lost because of strikes. In 1994, the figure was 280,000.

The average price of a house in London is more than double the average house price in Northern Ireland.

In 1961, £1 bought the same amount of goods as £11 in 1994.

SOURCE: Social Trends 1996,
Central Statistical Office, HMSO

TRINIDAD AND TOBAGO

What deductions can you make about the Caribbean islands of Trinidad and Tobago? Compare your deductions with those of others in the class.

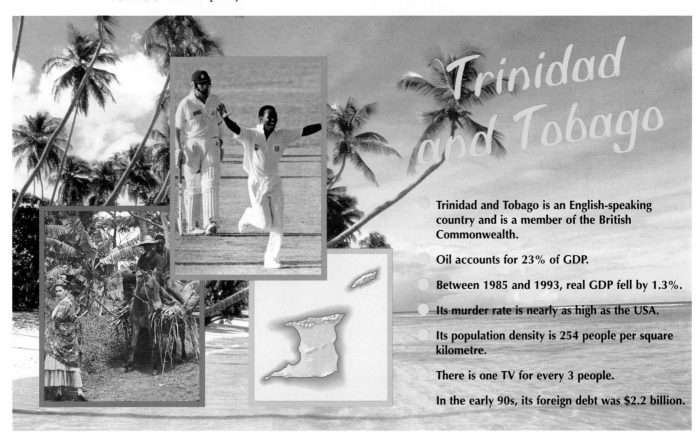

Trinidad and Tobago

- Trinidad and Tobago is an English-speaking country and is a member of the British Commonwealth.
- Oil accounts for 23% of GDP.
- Between 1985 and 1993, real GDP fell by 1.3%.
- Its murder rate is nearly as high as the USA.
- Its population density is 254 people per square kilometre.
- There is one TV for every 3 people.
- In the early 90s, its foreign debt was $2.2 billion.

PRACTICE

Work in small groups and write down a few unusual things to be found in your home or office. Then get others in the group to make a few deductions about you or your company.

Example   I've got a boomerang in my garage. → You must have been to Australia.
I always keep a towel in my desk drawer. → You must do sport at lunchtime.

doing **business** *Preparing a presentation*

Preparing a joint business presentation

THE MINI-COURSE ON PUBLIC SPEAKING

This is what the American writer Steven Silbiger writes about presentations (or public speaking) in his book, *The Ten Day MBA*.

THE MINI-COURSE
on Public Speaking

---

1 Know your audience.   Their interests, attention span.

2 Know your own capabilities. Can you deliver a joke?

3 Keep it simple.   Detailed information is best delivered in print.
                               Speeches should deliver concept and motivate.

---

1 According to Steven Silbiger, are the following true or false?

True or false?	T	F
You shouldn't allow the audience to influence what you say.		
You should always use humour in your presentations.		
Presentations should be about ideas.		
There should always be lots of facts and figures.		
Presentations should inspire people.		

2 Do you disagree with any of Stephen Silbiger's points? What extra advice would you give to someone who is making a business presentation for the first time?

PLANNING A PRESENTATION

Nearly all speakers plan their presentations carefully. Here are three ways of preparing a presentation.

1 Practise the presentation beforehand and then deliver it without notes.
2 Give the presentation from notes.
3 Write the presentation in full and read it.

1 What are the pros and cons of each approach?

2 Would you prepare a presentation in one of these ways? If not, describe how you would do it.

PREPARING VISUAL AIDS

1 Compare these two visual aids. Which do you think would be more effective on a screen during a presentation? Think about these points.

1 Which has more visual impact?
2 Which is easier to read?
3 Do you want people to read or to listen to you?

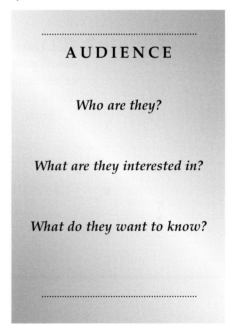

Audience

1 It is important that you know as much as possible about your audience.

2 You should try to find out who will be in the audience before the presentation starts. (Phone the organiser or speak to the boss!!)

3 You should also try to find out whatever you can about their interests. (You don't want to make jokes about soccer in a room full of Americans!)

4 Think about their attention span. Make sure that you don't give them too much information or spend too long on a subject which they find boring.

AUDIENCE

Who are they?

What are they interested in?

What do they want to know?

2 Decide how you would present this as a visual aid in a presentation. Write your own version.

```
When giving presentations, it is important to keep things
as simple as possible. If you have got lots of detailed
information, it is probably best to put it in print and
allow people to read it either before or after the
presentation. Presentations work best when they talk about
ideas rather than facts. They can also be good for
motivating and inspiring people. But, of course, that very
much depends on your personal qualities!
```

Compare your visual aid with those of others in the class.

doing **business** *Presentations: Openings and links*

COMPARING PRESENTATIONS

1 📼 Listen to the first presentation on the recording and, in small groups, discuss what is wrong with it. Make a list of your ideas.

2 📼 Listen to the second presentation on the recording and discuss in what ways it is better.

STARTING A PRESENTATION

📼 Listen to the second presentation again and answer these questions.

1 What is the purpose of the presentation?

2 These are the four main sections of the presentation. Put them in the correct order by completing the sentences underneath.

a some recommendations
b the current financial situation
c our prospects for the next twelve months
d our performance over the past year

Firstly, I want to talk about _____

Secondly, I'd like to examine _____

Thirdly, I'll look at _____

Finally, I'll make _____

3 When will the presenter answer questions?

4 Which of the phrases below does the presenter use to ...

a explain the purpose of the presentation
b describe the structure of the presentation
c say when she'll answer questions.

My main aim today is to tell you about our company's financial position.
I'll be happy to answer questions at the end of the presentation.
There are four parts to today's presentation.
I'm here today to tell you about our company's financial position.
I've divided my presentation into four parts.
I'll take questions at the end.

LINKS Here are four phrases that you can use to link the sections of your presentation together. Which phrase would you use ...

1	... before a summary?	*a*	Right. Let's recap, then.
2	... before the conclusion?		
3	... between any two points?	*b*	Let's move on, shall we?
4	... to introduce a visual aid?		
		c	I'd like you to have a look at this.
		d	I'd like to conclude by saying this.

PRESENTATION ROLES Use some of the phrases above to practise starting two presentations, based on the notes below.

Greet audience
Purpose : talk about new working practices
Four parts :
  1. Health and safety procedures
  2. Security measures
  3. Pay and conditions
  4. Management meetings
Questions at the end
Introduce bar chart

Greet audience
Purpose : talk about a new marketing campaign
Three parts :
  1. The product
  2. The launch
  3. Advertising and promotion
Questions during the presentation
Introduce graph

focus

Is profit the only goal?

BUSINESS GOALS

Is profit the only real goal of a company? In the United States, 47% say 'Yes', but most Japanese people think that other goals are more important. Work in small groups. Discuss these points:

1 Do you agree that profit is the only real goal of a company?

2 Here are some other possible goals of business. Circle the three which you think are the most important. Compare your choices.

> *to protect the environment*   to make products for customers
>
> **to provide a service to society**   *to develop new ideas*
>
> *to support government policies*   *to employ workers*

3 Add any other goals to the list that you think are important.

WHAT THE BOSSES SAY

Here is what four businesspeople say about the priorities of their businesses. Read the extracts and discuss these points in small groups.

1 For each person, decide which of these groups of people is the most important:

▌ shareholders	▌ customers	▌ society
▌ employees	▌ the community	▌ management

2 Which person has the shortest term view of business?

JOHN AKERS

'IBM exists to provide a return on invested capital to its stockholders.'

While John Akers was its boss, the American company IBM was the biggest computer company in the world. Akers left his job in January 1993.

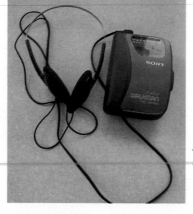

AKIO MORITA

'The investor and the employee are in the same position, but sometimes the employee is more important, because he will be there a long time, whereas an investor will often get in and out on a whim in order to make a profit.'

Akio Morita was the boss of Japan's giant Sony® Corporation. He introduced the Sony Walkman® to the world.

WALTER SCHUSSER

'Maximum profit for shareholders cannot be the essential aim of a company, because maximum profit today is not necessarily maximum profit for tomorrow. For us, economic performance and motivation are the basis of a company's capacity to perform socially.'

Walter Schusser is Vice President of Human Resources Management and Development for the German company Siemens.

ANITA RODDICK

'... the responsibility of business is not to create profits but to create organisations with a real commitment to the community. To do this business has to become a major educator of staff, customers and shareholders.'

▌ **GLOSSARY** ▌

a commitment
   a strong belief
educator
   a person or an organisation which teaches others

Anita Roddick and her husband started the British cosmetics company, the Body Shop, in 1976. It now has over 1,500 shops in around 40 countries.

WRITE YOUR OWN CREDO

General Robert Wood Johnson, who was once president of the American cosmetics company, Johnson & Johnson, summed up his view of business in the company credo.

Johnson & Johnson

CREDO

Service to customers comes first

Service to employees and management comes second

Service to the community comes third

Service to stockholders comes last

1 Write a similar piece that sums up your view of business.

2 In small groups, compare your 'credos' and explain your thinking behind them.

Parties!

INVITATIONS AND REPLIES

Mr & Mrs Edward Connor

request the pleasure of your company
for dinner

at 97 Kensington Close

on Friday 13 February

RSVP

7.30 for 8.00

rio beach hotel

Wednesday evening

Hugo,
Welcome to Rio! Hope you had a good flight. Would you like to go out for dinner on Friday night? Renata and I can pick you up at reception at around 7.00. We're out of town tomorrow, but you can fax me on my home number!

Paulo

Martha – do you fancy something to eat on Friday? What about the wine bar on the corner at 6.30?

Jethro.

1 Use these sentences to make appropriate replies to the three invitations above. (Two of the replies are refusals and one is an acceptance.)

> Thank you very much for your kind invitation to dinner on Friday.
> Dinner on Friday sounds great.
> Thanks for the invitation.
> I hope we get the chance to meet again some time soon.
> Sorry, I can't make it on Friday.
> I'm looking forward to seeing you again.
> Maybe another time?
> With best wishes
> I'm afraid that I will be unable to attend.

2 Now rewrite the three replies to make two acceptances and one refusal. Make any changes that are necessary.

3 Compare your answers.

PARTY TALK

Here are some things your host might say as he or she introduces you to guests at a business party.

1 In response to each, choose two sentences from this list.

> How are things?
> Congratulations!
> But it was delicious.
> That must have been fascinating.
> Did you get a chance to travel around the country?
> How are you finding the job?
> Where did you go?
> No, thanks.
> Pleased to meet you.
> Good to see you again.

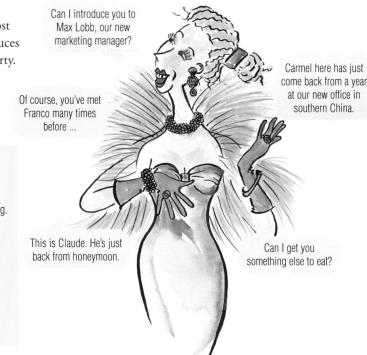

Can I introduce you to Max Lobb, our new marketing manager?

Carmel here has just come back from a year at our new office in southern China.

Of course, you've met Franco many times before ...

This is Claude. He's just back from honeymoon.

Can I get you something else to eat?

2 What other things could you say in this situation?

THE BONFIRE OF THE VANITIES

In his novel, *The Bonfire of the Vanities*, Tom Wolfe describes what happens when the Wall Street banker, Sherman McCoy, is invited to a formal dinner at an apartment on New York's Fifth Avenue.

Read the extract and answer the two questions underneath.

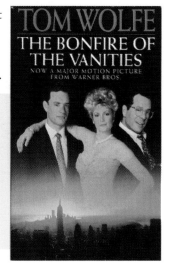

> Belatedly it occurred to Sherman that he should be talking to the woman on his left. Rawthrote, Mrs Rawthrote; who in the name of God was she? What could he say to her? He turned to his left – *and she was waiting.* She was staring straight at him, her laser eyes no more than eighteen inches from his face ... He opened his mouth ... he smiled ... he ransacked his brain for something to say ...

1 Which of these subjects do you think that Sherman should choose to start the conversation?

▌ her job
▌ the food
▌ the weather
▌ another person/other people at the party
▌ any other ideas?

2 What two questions could you ask Mrs Rawthrote about your chosen subject? Compare your subjects and questions.

BONFIRE ROLES

1 Take turns to be Sherman and Mrs Rawthrote in the situation above and develop the conversation.

2 To find out what Sherman actually said, turn to page 126.

business ethics

Ethical VOCABULARY

LAW, ETHICS AND COMMON SENSE

When you make judgements about business, you can use the law, you can use a set of moral principles (ethics), or you can use your own feelings (common sense). Here are some adjectives you can use when you're making these kinds of judgements.

THE LAW		ETHICS		COMMON SENSE	
+	–	+	–	+	–
legal		moral		honest	
just		ethical		fair	

Add *un-*, *im-*, *il-* or *dis-* to the beginning of each adjective in the table to make words which have the opposite meaning and compare your answers.

THE LAW

1 Here are four activities which are against the law in many countries. Match each activity to its definition, by writing the appropriate letter in the middle column.

CRIME	DEFINITION	VERB
bribery		to bribe
theft		to steal
fraud		to defraud
deception		to deceive

a the crime of taking someone's property
b making someone accept that something which is false or bad is true or good
c unfairly influencing someone by giving them money or gifts
d dishonest behaviour for the purpose of making money

2 Quickly read the text opposite and find one (or more) activity that *could* match each of the crimes above. (Remember that there is lots of room for interpretation in all legal systems!)

3 🗣 Compare your answers with a partner.

4 🗣 Which of the activities described opposite are illegal in your country/countries?

ETHICS

1 Look again at the text and make a list of activities which you think are immoral.

2 🗣 Compare your lists and give reasons for your choices.

COMMON SENSE

Are there any activities opposite which you think are not illegal or immoral but which shouldn't be allowed? Discuss your ideas with your partner and give your reasons.

SUN TZU AND MANAGEMENT

This extract comes from Khoo Kheng-Hor's book *Sun Tzu and Management*. Sun Tzu was an ancient Chinese military strategist whose ideas are still seen as relevant to the modern business world.

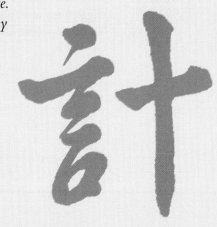

This is the area commonly known as industrial espionage. Although some people have condemned such activities, my personal feeling is that all is fair in war.

The following shows some of the ways one can obtain information from men who know the enemy position:

1 *Getting information from potential recruits*

In the past when conducting job interviews, I found some applicants ... would often unknowingly or even deliberately become invaluable sources of information.

2 *Conducting false job interviews*

Here the intention is not really to employ but rather to get the selected candidates to talk and hopefully reveal some useful information.

3 *Hiring people away from competitors*

A deliberate 'headhunting' activity.

4 *Deliberately planting spies in a competitor's firm*

There have been cases where a person leaves his organization to join a competitor for a while before returning to his original organization.

5 *Encouraging key customers to talk*

From my experience, key customers such as my wholesalers and industrial buyers are always more than ready to talk.

6 *Interviewing competitors*

A way of interviewing your competitors is to pretend to be a potential customer or supplier.

7 *Taking factory tours*

Highly trained and observant engineers have been known to take in what they see and reproduce blueprints after visiting their competitors' factories.

8 *Taking competitors' products apart*

Some companies spend years in research and development activities. But the moment they put a new product on the market, you can buy it, take it apart and improve on it.

9 *Buying competitors' garbage*

A disgusting business but high returns for the enemy if one is not too careful what one throws into the wastepaper baskets!

▌ **GLOSSARY** ▌

industrial espionage
   spying on another company
blueprints   *plans*
garbage   *rubbish*

AND FINALLY ...   **1** Choose adjectives from the table on the opposite page to describe each of the nine activities on the list in the article.

2 Compare and discuss your conclusions with the rest of the class.

G R A M M A R   R E V I E W

THE HOOVER FIASCO

1 Read this article about one of the biggest business mistakes of the 1990s and choose your answers to these two questions.

1 What would you have done if you had heard about Hoover's special offer?

I would have ...

... ignored it.

... bought £100 vacuum cleaner and applied for free flights.

... bought £100 vacuum cleaner, applied for free flights and then sold the vacuum cleaner on the secondhand market.

... bought as many vacuum cleaners as possible and applied for as many free flights as possible.

2 If you had applied for free flights, but hadn't been given them, what would you have done?

I would have ...

... ignored it.

... complained to the company.

... taken legal action.

... gone to a consumer advice organisation.

2 🗣 Explain the reasons for your choices.

HOOVER'S FREE FLIGHTS FIASCO

Hoover has been the top brand in vacuum cleaners for so long that the verb 'to hoover' has become a part of the everyday English language. But towards the end of 1992, a sales promotion in the UK brought the company to the edge of disaster.

In an attempt to boost its sales, Hoover offered its British customers two flights to continental Europe or the USA free with any purchase over £100. It didn't take a genius to realise that flights like these were worth much more than £100 and before long more than 600,000 people had bought a Hoover product and applied for its special offer.

Clearly, Hoover had made a massive error of judgement. A huge market for secondhand Hoovers quickly developed as people bought their products just to take advantage of the special offer. Before long many began to doubt whether the company would ever be able to honour its promises.

In the end, 220,000 people got free flights – at a cost to the company of £48 million. But many more were disappointed and Hoover attracted an enormous amount of bad publicity, as angry customers took legal action.

As profits slumped, Hoover's European president and two senior executives lost their jobs. In the middle of 1995, Hoover's European operations were sold to the Italian company Candy for just over £100 million.

Hoover® is a registered trademark

▌ CHECK

When you're speculating about something in the past that didn't happen, use this kind of construction (called a 'third conditional').

If I *had heard* about the offer, I *would   have   bought* a Hoover.
   past perfect   would + have + past participle

When you're talking about a possibility, use *could* or *might* instead of *would*.

I could have bought a hundred vacuum cleaners.

And when you're giving your opinion about the past or talking about an idea that you think is morally correct, use *should*.

I should never have stolen that vacuum cleaner.

▌ *For more on the third conditional, turn to page 130* ▌

PRONUNCIATION

In normal speech, some of the sounds in third conditional sentences are elided (left out).

1 Listen to the three ways that this sentence is pronounced on the tape.
If I had heard about the offer, I would have bought the vacuum cleaner.

2 Pronounce your answers to questions 1 and 2 in the Hoover section oppposite in three different ways.

HOOVER'S REACTION

1 When Hoover realised that 600,000 people had applied for its special offer, what could the company have done? Listen to the two people on the tape discussing Hoover's options. Tick the ideas that they mention.

1 say the special offer was a joke

2 delay a decision for as long as possible

3 offer a different (and cheaper) gift to all the applicants

4 get legal help immediately

5 give all the applicants their free flights

6 offer one free flight instead of two

7 apologise and say the offer was a mistake

8 wait and forget

2 Write sentences from the ideas on the list, using the third conditional.

3 Explain what you would have done if you had been Hoover's boss in this situation.

THREE MORE BUSINESS PROBLEMS

Discuss these three real situations from business history. What would you have done in these business situations from the past? Compare your ideas with those of others in the class. To find out what actually happened, turn to page 126.

In 1846, an American called Elias Howe invented the sewing machine – but it seemed that in the USA no one wanted it. He travelled to England and tried to get people interested, but again he was a failure. However, when he returned to the USA he discovered that a man called Isaac Singer had stolen his patent, started a factory and was making a huge amount of money from his invention.

What would you have done, if you'd been Elias Howe?

In 1983, Coca-Cola announced that it had changed the recipe of the best-selling soft drink in the world. Two months later research showed that 80% of people thought that the change had been a bad idea.

What action would you have recommended if you had been a part of Coca-Cola's top management?

In 1990, the French company Perrier discovered that there were traces of a poisonous substance called benzene in some of its bottled water.

What do you think the company should have done in that situation?

doing **business** *Using rhetoric*

HOW TO GET AHEAD IN ADVERTISING

The film *How To Get Ahead In Advertising* starts with part of a formal presentation given by an advertising executive called Bagley. The script below is from the middle of his presentation. Read it and answer these questions.

1 What are Best Company supermarkets worried about?
2 How would you describe the kind of food that Best Co sells?
3 What do you think that Best Co wants the advertising agency to do?
4 What is Bagley's opinion of the British sausage?

Let me try and clarify some of this for you. Best Company supermarkets are not interested in selling wholesome foods. They are not worried about the nation's health. What is concerning them is that the nation appears to be getting worried about its health. And that is what's worrying Best Co. Because Best Co wants to go on selling them what it always has, i.e. the white breads, baked beans, canned foods and that suppurating, fat-squirting little heart attack traditionally known as the British sausage. So, how can we help them with that?

Richard E. Grant as Bagley

GLOSSARY

wholesome *healthy*
suppurating, fat-squirting,
little heart attack
    *horrible, greasy, unhealthy
    kind of food*

SIGNPOSTING

Many business presenters introduce each step of their presentation.

1 Which one of the five things in the table below does Bagley introduce in the first line of the extract?

a visual aid	
a digression	
an example	
an important opinion	
a point of clarification	

2 Match these four sentences to the remaining four things in the table.

a I'd like to give you an example.
b What I'm getting at is this.
c Let's have a look at this.
d To move off the point for a moment ...

3 Which of the above phrases would you use to introduce each of the four extracts on the recording?

4 Compare your answers.

A LIST OF THREE

1 Look at the script again and answer these questions.

  1 What two things are Best Co not concerned about?
  2 What *are* they concerned about?
  3 Why do you think that Bagley introduces his point in this way?

2 🎞 Listen to the next two extracts. Both speakers use a list of three in their presentations. Just like Bagley's presentation, their lists follow this pattern: *not x ... not y ... but z.* Summarise what you hear in this table.

	SPEAKER 1	SPEAKER 2
Not ...		
Not ...		
But ...		

3 Work with a partner and write a short paragraph using the *not x, not y, but z* pattern to express these ideas.

  ▌ Your company needs both excellent products and excellent customer service.
  ▌ Your company is offering its customers a discount of 50% on its main product.

RHETORICAL QUESTIONS

1 Both the extracts on the recording end with questions. One is a 'rhetorical question' – that the speaker answers; the other is a question for the audience. Listen again and decide which is which.

2 Look again at the end of the extract from Bagley's presentation. What kind of question does he ask?

3 Return to the two lists of three you made above. Think of a question that you could use to conclude each list.

PRESENTATION ROLES

👥 Use some of the phrases and ideas above to practise extracts from these two presentations, based on the notes below.

1. Signpost an important opinion.

2. Use a list of three to say that your company is not interested in present or past results but only in future results.

3. Ask a question about how this will be done.

1. Signpost an example.

2. Use a list of three to say that in the past year your company has increased profits by 50%.

3. Ask a question about how this has been done.

doing **business** *Delivery*

GREED IS GOOD
In the film *Wall Street*, the New York financier, Gordon Gekko, makes a famous speech to the shareholders of a company called Teldar Paper.

1 Read the speech and then, working in pairs, try to sum up its message in your own words. (Don't worry if you can't understand every word: just try to summarise its general meaning.)

2 In small groups, discuss if you agree with Gekko's main idea.

The point is, ladies and gentlemen, that greed, for lack of a better word, is good. Greed is right. Greed works. Greed clarifies, cuts through and captures the essence of the evolutionary spirit. Greed, in all its forms – for life, for money, for love, for knowledge – has marked the upward surge of mankind. And greed, you mark my words, will not only save Teldar Paper, but that other malfunctioning corporation called the USA.

▌ GLOSSARY ▌

for lack of a better word
  because there is no better word
captures the essence
  sums up
the upward surge
  the development
you mark my words
  listen to what I say
malfunctioning corporation
  a company that is not working properly

REPETITION
Many speakers use repetition to help them put their message across. Look at Gekko's speech and find the following:

1 a word that is repeated
2 a pattern of words that is repeated
3 a sound that is repeated.

EMPHASIS

1 In English, speakers also use their voices to draw attention to the key ideas in their speeches. Underline the three words in this sentence that you would emphasise.
'The point is, ladies and gentlemen, that greed, for lack of a better word, is good.'

2  Compare your ideas about emphasis with the way that the actor says the sentence.

3 Practise saying the above sentence out loud, in the same way as the actor on the tape.

PAUSES

1 Obviously, you need to make brief pauses while you talk, but how should you time your pauses? Which of these options would you choose?

  a Pause only when you need to breathe.
  b Pause at regular intervals.
  c Pause according to the meaning of what you say.

2 Here are three ways of pausing during part of the first sentence of the speech. Work in pairs and say them aloud to each other. Which way do you think is best?

  a greed for lack/of a better word is/good
  b greed/for lack of a better word/is good
  c greed for lack/of a better/word is good

3 Check by listening again to how the actor pauses.

THE VOICE

1 What is the best way to stand so that you can speak in a relaxed way? Try saying a few words in these two positions.

2 Which of these three parts of the body does an actor imagine that the voice comes from?

Try saying a few words while imagining that your voice is coming from each of these three places.

a mouth
b throat
c diaphragm

GEKKO ROLES

1 Look again at Gekko's speech. Underline the key words that you want to emphasise and mark the places where you are going to pause. Now, work in groups and take turns to deliver Gekko's speech while the other group members give feedback on your performance.

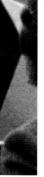

focus

Levi Strauss & Co.

Robert D. Haas

Levi Strauss & Co. is not just famous for the jeans and casual clothing that it makes. In the business world it is also known as a company that is run according to strict ethical principles. But, as Levi's Chief Executive, Robert D. Haas, says, doing business like this is not always easy.

'We are far from perfect. We are far from where we want to be. But the goal is out there and it is worth striving for.'

Here are two incidents from its recent history. Read them and then in small groups, discuss what you would have done.

LEVI'S AND CHILD LABOUR

1 Before you read the text, discuss these points.

1 What are the arguments against the use of child labour?

2 Are there any situations in which child labour is acceptable?

2 Now read the text and answer these questions.

1 Why did child labour become an issue for Levi's in 1992?

2 What are the arguments in favour of child labour in this situation?

3 What would you have done, if you had been a member of the Levi's management team faced with this dilemma?

> 'We will conduct our business ethically and demonstrate leadership in satisfying our responsibilities to our communities and to society.'
>
> *(from the Levi Strauss & Co. Mission Statement)*

In 1992, to meet the requirements of its own ethical code, Levi's began taking action on child labour violations, by enforcing a ban on employment of children under the age of 14. Two Bangladeshi contractors admitted to Levi's that they hired children and agreed to fire them.

They also argued to Levi's officials, however, that the girls and boys provided their families' only economic support – most of them were the only children in large, single-parent families.

'We don't support child labour,' says Robert H. Dunn, Levi's corporate-communications and community-affairs chief. 'But our intention is not to have a devastating effect on families.'

Levi's could have ignored its code or it could have fired the kids ...

Business Week, September 12 1994

3 To find out what Levi's actually did, turn to page 126 and then, in small groups, discuss whether Levi's acted according to the principle in the Mission Statement above.

LEVI'S AND THE FACTORY CLOSURE

1 Before you read the text discuss these points in small groups.

1 In business, whose interests are more important: a company's shareholders or its employees?

2 Should a company manufacture its products in its own country or in the country which has the lowest costs?

> 'We want our people to feel respected, treated fairly, listened to and involved.'
>
> *(From the Levi Strauss & Co. Aspiration Statement)*

2 Now read the text and answer these questions.

1 Why did Levi's close its San Antonio factory?

2 Does it matter that Levi's faced a storm of protest?

3 What would you have done if you had been a member of Levi's management team in this situation?

> The trouble began in January 1990, when Levi's management announced the closure of a large factory in San Antonio, Texas, which employed 1,115 workers. The factory, which had been purchased from another firm in the early 1980s, wasn't operating as efficiently as Levi's wanted, so the company decided to move its production to other US facilities and to subcontract to factories in Costa Rica, where labour costs were a fraction of those in San Antonio.
>
> A senior vice-president from San Francisco delivered the news to San Antonio workers on the morning of January 17 and started a storm of protest that continued for years afterwards.
>
> The Frontiers of Excellence, *Robert Waterman*

3 Again, to find out what Levi's actually did, turn to page 126. In small groups, discuss whether Levi's acted according to the principle in the Aspiration Statement above.

A PRESENTATION

1 Choose one of the two Levi's case studies as the basis for a short presentation. Your presentation could follow this pattern.

1 introduction

2 a brief summary of the case study

3 a brief summary of the issues discussed by your group

4 conclusion (your own views).

2 Work in small groups and take turns to give your presentations.

social skills

Gifts

THE LOCKHEED SCANDAL

In the mid 1970s, the Saudi Arabian businessman, Adnan Khashoggi, became famous for his role in a major business scandal. It was said that in five years he received $106 million in commissions from the American company, Lockheed. Here is a brief description of his business style.

Read the article and then talk about these questions in small groups.

1 What do you think is meant by the idea that there is no distinction between business and hospitality? Do you agree?
2 How would you have reacted if you had been one of his visitors in Paris?
3 Can you think of any similar examples of this style of doing business?

> **K**HASHOGGI'S attitude to business and hospitality was that there was no basic distinction between the two ... In Paris his visitors would find themselves caught up in his 'cast of thousands' with attentive executives ... To some of the senior executives, Khashoggi showed a hospitality which seemed almost magical. A private plane just happened to be waiting at the airport to fly them to some resort: Khashoggi's yacht just happened to be waiting ...
>
> The Observer, *14.3.76*

INVITATIONS AND OFFERS

1 Put these sentences into the appropriate column.

a Can I invite you to dinner this evening?
b This is a small token of our gratitude.
c Thank you. That's very kind of you.
d Thanks very much for everything. I'd like you to have this.
e That's very kind of you, but I must refuse.
f I'm sorry but my company doesn't allow me to accept gifts.
g Would you like to go to the concert tonight?

INVITATIONS AND OFFERS	ACCEPTANCES	REFUSALS

2 Can you think of any other appropriate phrases?

SOUNDING POLITE

Listen to three short conversations based on some of the phrases above. Although all the speakers are using polite phrases, they sometimes sound rude. In each case, decide whether you think the speakers are being rude or polite.

GIFTS AND ETHICS   You are on a business trip to visit one of your company's suppliers. Which of the things below would you accept and which would you refuse? Work in small groups and explain your reasons.

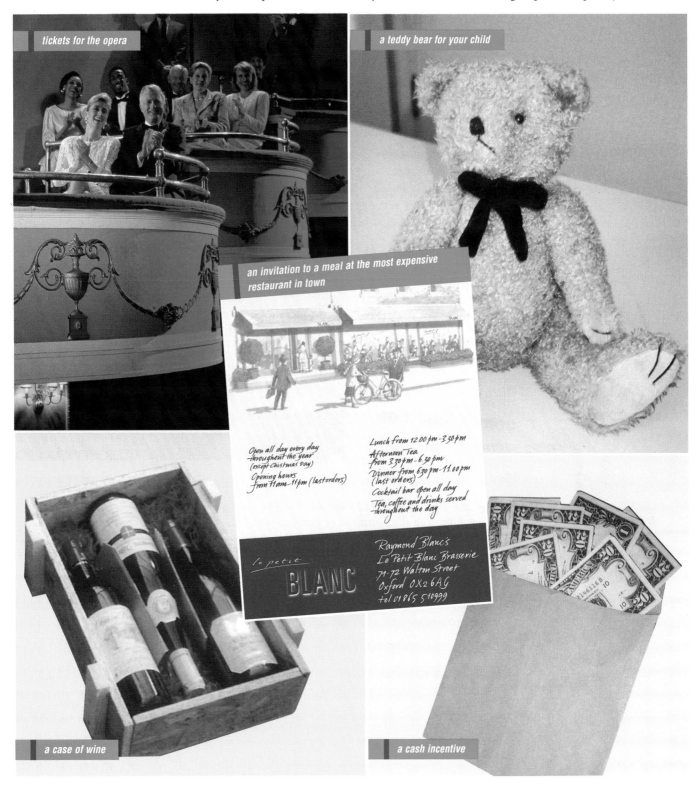

tickets for the opera

a teddy bear for your child

an invitation to a meal at the most expensive restaurant in town

Open all day every day throughout the year (except Christmas Day)
Opening hours from 11am–11pm (last orders)

Lunch from 12.00 pm – 3.30 pm
Afternoon Tea from 3.30 pm – 6.30 pm
Dinner from 6.30 pm – 11.00 pm (last orders)
Cocktail bar open all day
Tea, coffee and drinks served throughout the day

le petit
BLANC
Raymond Blanc's
Le Petit Blanc Brasserie
71-72 Walton Street
Oxford OX2 6AG
tel 01865 510999

a case of wine

a cash incentive

GIVING ROLES   Have five conversations based on the five gifts above. Take turns to offer/invite and accept/refuse, using the phrases above and others that you know. Then try to finish the conversation in an appropriate way.

10 the **digital revolution**

Hi-tech VOCABULARY

A REVOLUTION IN BUSINESS

Tom Peters is probably the most influential management thinker in the world. He says we live in 'crazy times' and 'crazy times call for crazy organizations'.

This painting shows what he thinks of a crazy organization.

In small groups discuss: What does he mean? Think about these issues:

power creativity

communication

control hierarchy

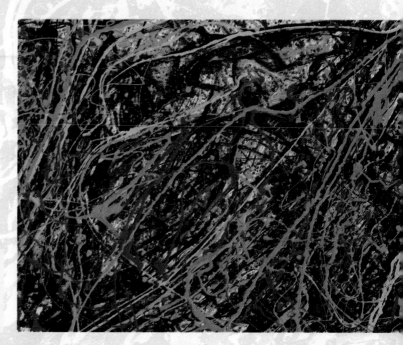

(Tom Peters' explanation is on page 126.)

A REVOLUTION IN LANGUAGE

Major revolutions in the industrial or business world also produce changes in language. Here are some examples of the way the digital revolution is changing the English language.

Fill in the gaps using the definitions underneath.

WORD	ORIGINAL MEANING	NEW MEANING
to boot	to kick	
a bug		an error in a computer program
to crack	to make something split	
a flame		an insulting or unfriendly e-mail
a geek	an entertainer who bites the heads off live chickens	
a pirate		a person who illegally copies software
to surf	to ride on a board on the waves of the sea	

to move around the Internet   a person who robs ships at sea   to start a computer   to break a computer code
a small insect   a red or yellow burning gas   a rich successful person in the computer industry

**TECHNOLOGIES AND
SERVICES**

1 Read what J.B. Morgan, the Chief executive of IBM UK wrote about the digital revolution.

'That we are in the midst of a new revolution must be obvious to everyone. There is a revolution in the technologies: ... There is a revolution in the services being offered: ... In many ways the communications revolution has only just begun.'

J.B. Morgan Chief Executive, IBM United Kingdom

2 In the gaps in the article above, J.B. Morgan listed the technologies and services which were in a state of revolution. Which of these do you think he called technologies and which did he call services? Write them in the appropriate column.

television	video-conferencing	optical fibre	cable TV
interactive television	digital telephony	the Internet	telephone marketing
mobile radio	satellite broadcasting		

TECHNOLOGIES	SERVICES

3 Add to the list other technologies and services which you think are in the middle of a revolution.

WORD STRESS

1 Listen to this phrase.

Notice that the main stress falls on 'soft', marked ' and the secondary stress falls on 'in' marked , .

the 'software ,industry

2 Listen to the way the phrases above are stressed. Try to mark the main stress and secondary stress in each case.

3 Take turns to say the words to each other, getting the main stress and the secondary stress in the right place.

**THE REVOLUTION
AND YOU**

1 Which technologies have had the biggest impact on your business life over recent years? Explain why.

2 Which technologies will have the greatest effect over the next ten years? Again, explain why.

GRAMMAR REVIEW

A BAD PREDICTION

Many years ago, Thomas Watson, the founder of IBM, made this prediction.

'I think there is a world market for about five computers.'

How would you report this statement to another person?
Cross out the two sentences which you think are not correct.

▮ He says there is a world market for about five computers.
▮ He said there was a market for about five computers.
▮ He said there had been a market for about five computers.

CHECK

If the reporting verb is a past tense, the verb in the other clause moves one tense back.

'I'm leaving.' ➡ He said he was leaving.

If you're talking about the future, use *would* in the other clause.

'I will see you tomorrow.' ➡ He said he would see me tomorrow.

If the reporting verb is in the present, there's no change.

'I can't do it today.' ➡ He says he can't do it today.

▮ *For more on reported speech, turn to page 144* ▮

Thomas Watson

SOME MORE QUOTATIONS

1 Here are some more thoughts people have had in the past, on the digital world. Put them into reported speech.

The computer industry, as an industry, has never made a dime.

1   Peter Drucker, management thinker

Finance is a pure information-processing game. A lot of people in the business are doing things that should be done by computers.

THE WEB IS NOT GOING TO CHANGE THE WORLD, CERTAINLY NOT IN THE NEXT TEN YEARS.

2   Steve Jobs, the man who founded Apple

3   David Shaw, Wall Street financier and computer expert

What's really exciting about the digital revolution is that everyone is going to have a computer.

4   Steven Holtzmann, writer and digital entrepreneur

2 Which of the quotations do you agree or disagree with? Explain why.

Reported speech

THE GEORGE LUCAS INTERVIEW

In an interview with *Wired* magazine, George Lucas, the film director and creator of *Star Wars*, talks about the impact of digital technology on the film industry.

1 Quickly read the interview and answer these questions.

1 When will George Lucas make a digital movie?

2 What advantage of digital movie-making is mentioned?

3 How important is this development in the history of the film industry?

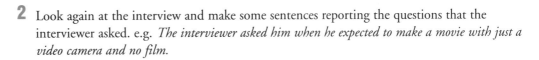

WIRED	Everything seems to be going digital. When do you expect to make a movie using just a video camera and no film?
LUCAS	In two or three years.
WIRED	The new films will be cheaper, too. What will your new *Star Wars* movies cost?
LUCAS	I'm hoping to do the new *Star Wars* films for between US$60 and US$70 million. These are maybe $120 to $140 million movies.
WIRED	That's amazing. How are you making it so cheaply?
LUCAS	The first film will be a big experiment. Some of it is going to work; some of it is not. We're going out there in a whole different style of film-making.
WIRED	Is this approach revolutionary?
LUCAS	Digital technology is the same revolution as adding sound to pictures and the same revolution as adding colour to pictures. Nothing more and nothing less.

George Lucas, film director and creator of Star Wars

2 Look again at the interview and make some sentences reporting the questions that the interviewer asked. e.g. *The interviewer asked him when he expected to make a movie with just a video camera and no film.*

3 Now make sentences reporting what George Lucas said. e.g. *He said that he would make a digital movie in the next two or three years.*

PRACTICE

1 Write a questionnaire of five or more questions, asking about the digital revolution (e.g. How has it affected your life? How will it change business over the next ten years?).

2 Visit someone from another 'pair' and take turns to ask and answer the questions on the questionnaire. Make notes on the other person's replies.

3 Return to your original pair and report back. (He said it hadn't changed his life much. She didn't think it would have a big effect on business.)

doing **business** *e-mail 1*

MICROSERFS   *Microserfs* is a novel about a group of young computer programmers who work for the giant software company, Microsoft. Here, one of the characters talks about his experience of e-mail.

1 Read the piece and answer these questions.

1 Why are so many e-mail messages sent at Microsoft?
2 What advantage does e-mail have over answerphone messages?
3 How much of his e-mail does the writer read?

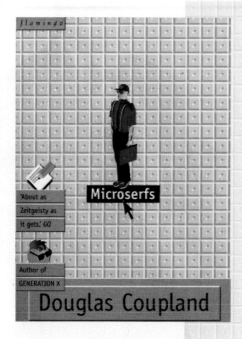

↗ I've been thinking: I get way too many pieces of e-mail, about sixty a day. This is a typical number at Microsoft. E-mail is like highways – if you have them, traffic follows.

↗ I'm an e-mail addict. Everybody at Microsoft is an addict. The future of e-mail usage is being pioneered right here. The cool thing with e-mail is when you send it, there's no possibility of connecting with the person on the other end. It's better than phone answering machines because, with them, the person on the other line might actually pick up the phone and you might have to talk.

↗ Typically, everybody has about a 40% immediate cull rate – those pieces of mail you can delete immediately because of a frivolous tag line. What you read of the remaining 60% depends on how much of a life you have. The less of a life, the more mail you read.

▌ GLOSSARY ▌

way too many	*far too many*
cool thing	*good thing*
cull rate	*rate of deletion*
frivolous tag line	
	unimportant title

2 How does this compare with your experience of e-mail? Talk about these questions.

1 How many pieces of e-mail do you get a day?
2 What percentage of this is useful to you?
3 What percentage of your messages do you delete immediately?
4 What percentage do you read?
5 What percentage do you save?
6 Do you prefer to write an e-mail or to leave an answerphone message? Explain why.

E-MAIL AND CHANGE

1 How do you think that e-mail has changed business life? Choose the statement from each of these pairs which comes closest to your opinion.

2 In small groups, compare your choices.

3 What do you think are the three most important ways in which e-mail has changed the way we work?

e-mail saves time.
It wastes time.

e-mail means that people spend more time at their desks.
It allows people to have a more flexible working life.

e-mail is now more important than the telephone.
It could never be more important than the telephone.

TWO VIEWS 📼 Listen to two professional people talking about the effect of e-mail on business life.

1 Which of the above six statements you have just discussed do you think that each of them would agree or disagree with?

◀ *Alan Davies is an information technology trainer for the oil company, Shell International.*

▼ *Susan Fearn is a radio producer for the international broadcasting organisation, BBC World Service.*

2 👥 Who said each of the things below?

▮ When I first started using e-mail back in '86, I really just used it to transmit simple text messages.

▮ I understand that some organisations are establishing e-mail filters.

▮ This product is not just text, it is digital information.

▮ In my view, e-mail is very definitely a mixed blessing.

▮ Probably 75% of the e-mails that I get are not directly relevant.

▮ The other thing that is happening now is the mobile office.

📼 Check your answers by listening again.

E-MAIL AND YOU **1** In small groups, discuss what you think are the advantages and disadvantages of e-mail.

2 Write an e-mail message of no more than 100 words summarising your view of the way that e-mail is changing working life.

3 👥 Compare your messages.

doing **business** *e-mail 2*

EFFECTIVE WRITING   There are no rules for writing e-mail messages in English. But it will probably help if you write clearly and concisely. However, the English writer, George Orwell, gave these rules for writing effectively.

1 Read the rules and then check your comprehension with the true/false activity.

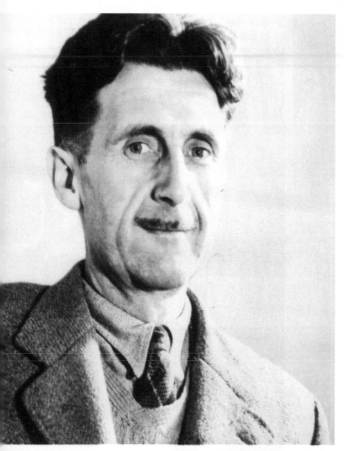

George Orwell

THE RULES OF EFFECTIVE WRITING

Never use a metaphor, simile or other figure of speech which you are used to seeing in print.

Never use a long word when a short one will do.

If it is possible to cut a word out, always cut it out.

Never use the passive where you can use the active.

Never use a foreign phrase, a scientific word or a jargon word if you can think of an everyday English equivalent.

Break any of these rules sooner than say anything outright barbarous.

True or false?   T   F

1 Use clichés as often as possible.

2 Try to use short words.

3 Delete words where possible.

4 Base your sentences on this word order: subject – verb – object.

5 Avoid ordinary everyday English.

6 Never break any of these rules.

2 According to Orwell's rules, what is wrong with these sentences?

  1 One of our highly-qualified, dynamic sales and marketing representatives will make your acquaintance over the next two weeks.

  2 You will be visited by one of our salespeople during the next two weeks.

3 How do you think that George Orwell would rewrite these two sentences?

EDITING ACTIVITY **1** 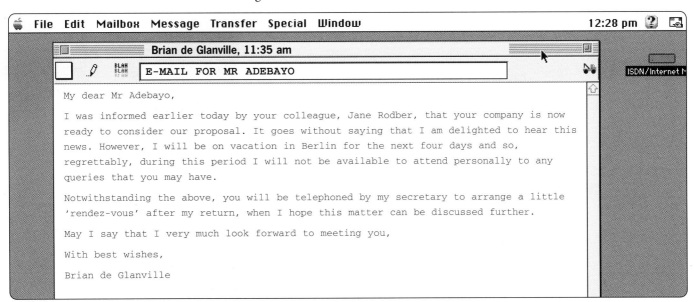 Delete as many unnecessary words as possible from this e-mail message, while keeping the meaning.

File   Edit   Mailbox   Message   Transfer   Special   Window   12:28 pm

Brian de Glanville, 11:35 am

E-MAIL FOR MR ADEBAYO   ISDN/Internet M

My dear Mr Adebayo,

I was informed earlier today by your colleague, Jane Rodber, that your company is now ready to consider our proposal. It goes without saying that I am delighted to hear this news. However, I will be on vacation in Berlin for the next four days and so, regrettably, during this period I will not be available to attend personally to any queries that you may have.

Notwithstanding the above, you will be telephoned by my secretary to arrange a little 'rendez-vous' after my return, when I hope this matter can be discussed further.

May I say that I very much look forward to meeting you,

With best wishes,

Brian de Glanville

2 Rewrite the remaining text according to Orwell's rules. (Change foreign words to English ones, change passive verbs into active ones, etc.)

3 Compare your version to the version on page 126. Which do you think is better? Explain why.

WRITING REPLIES Write e-mails in reply to the following messages. Compare your replies with those of your colleagues.

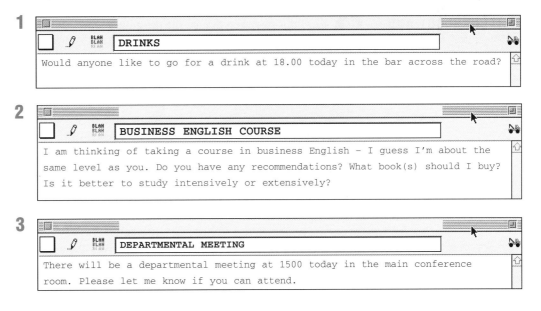

1

DRINKS

Would anyone like to go for a drink at 18.00 today in the bar across the road?

2

BUSINESS ENGLISH COURSE

I am thinking of taking a course in business English – I guess I'm about the same level as you. Do you have any recommendations? What book(s) should I buy? Is it better to study intensively or extensively?

3

DEPARTMENTAL MEETING

There will be a departmental meeting at 1500 today in the main conference room. Please let me know if you can attend.

CHAIN E-MAIL Work in groups of three. One person in the group should write a short message of around 30 words and pass it to the person sitting next to him or her. This person should summarise the message in less than 20 words and pass it to the next person. This person should sum up the message in less than 10 words and give it to the person who started the chain. Compare the first message with the final message and discuss how much of the meaning has been lost.

focus

The digital future

Nicholas Negroponte is director of the Media Laboratory at the Massachusetts Institute of Technology. Here are a few ideas from his book, *Being Digital.*

TECHNOLOGY AND CHANGE

Discuss these three ideas in small groups.

1 If a doctor from the middle of the nineteenth century walked into a modern hospital, how many pieces of equipment would he or she recognise? Most of the equipment? Some of it? Or almost none at all? Explain.

2 If a teacher from the middle of the nineteenth century walked into a modern classroom, how different would the technology be? Look round your own classroom and find things that he or she would find difficult to use.

Nicholas Negroponte

3 If a teacher and a doctor of today went forward just ten years in time, how much more different do you think their jobs would be?

TECHNOLOGY AND VALUE

Read this story and discuss the three questions.

I recently visited the headquarters of one of America's top five integrated circuit manufacturers. I was asked to sign in and, in the process, was asked whether I had a laptop computer with me. Of course I did. The receptionist asked for the model and serial number and for its value.

'Roughly between one and two million dollars,' I said.

'Oh, that cannot be, sir,' she replied. 'What do you mean? Let me see it.'

I showed her my old Powerbook and she estimated its value at $2000.

1 Why do you think that Negroponte's estimate of his computer's value is so different from the receptionist's?

2 Whose estimate do you think is closer to the computer's true value?

3 What does this tell you about the value of things in the old world and the value of things in the digital world?

TECHNOLOGY AND CONTENT

Here is a conversation between President John F. Kennedy, his scientific adviser, Jerry Wiesner, and Vladimir Zworykin, one of the scientists who developed television technology. Read it and then, in small groups, discuss:

1 What is the point of the story?
2 What do you find more impressive about the digital age: the technology or the content? Give examples to support your answer.

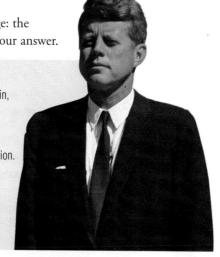

WIESNER	Mr President, I'd like you to meet Vladimir Zworykin, the man who got you elected.
JFK	How is that?
WIESNER	Well, Mr Zworykin is the man who invented television.
JFK	That's a wonderful achievement, Mr Zworykin.
ZWORYKIN	You can't have watched much TV recently, Mr President.

John F. Kennedy

A DIGITAL ASSISTANT?

Here, Negroponte describes a business dinner with Nobutaka Shikanai, a very wealthy Japanese businessman and art collector. Read the story and then, in small groups, discuss these questions.

1 What is so good about Mr Shikanai's private secretary?
2 What characteristics would Negroponte's ideal personal computer have?
3 What would your ideal digital assistant be like?

'At dinner with Mr and Mrs Shikanai, we were joined by Mr Shikanai's private male secretary who, quite significantly, spoke perfect English ... The conversation was started by Wiesner, who expressed great interest in the work of the artist, Alexander Calder. The secretary listened to the story and then translated it from beginning to end, with Mr Shikanai listening attentively. Mr Shikanai reflected, paused and then looked up at us and said "Ohhhh."

The male secretary then translated: "Mr Shikanai says that he too is very impressed with the work of Calder and Mr Shikanai's most recent acquisitions were made under the circumstances of ..."

Wait a minute. Where did all that come from?

... I said to myself that night if I really want to build a personal computer, it has to be as good as Mr Shikanai's secretary.'

Polite excuses

PRETTY WOMAN

In the film, *Pretty Woman*, a businessman, Edward Lewis, takes his girlfriend, Vivian, to meet Jim Morse, the boss of a large American corporation and his grandson, David (who also holds an important position in the company). Over dinner, they discuss a future business deal and David Morse accuses Edward Lewis of working with corrupt politicians. Below is how the conversation ends.

1 Do the people in the scene finish on good or bad terms?
2 Do you think that the final line in the scene is serious, ironic or humorous? What else could Edward Lewis say in that situation?

Richard Gere plays Edward Lewis

LEWIS	There will be no contract. The contract is buried in Appropriations Committee and it will remain there.
DAVID MORSE	And how the hell did you pull something like that? What, you ... you got dirty politicians in your pockets now or something?
JIM MORSE	Easy, easy, calm down, calm down, David. Mr Lewis plays hardball.
LEWIS	Yes, yes I do.
DAVID MORSE	I've heard enough of this. Vivian, it was a great pleasure to meet you. I'm sorry, grandfather, I've got to get some air.
JIM MORSE	(*To Mr Lewis*) I'd better join my grandson. You two enjoy your dinner, I'm sure it'll be delicious. (*To Vivian*) Good luck, miss. (*To Lewis*) Watch out, Lewis, I'm going to tear you apart.
LEWIS	I look forward to it, sir.

▌ GLOSSARY ▌

the Appropriations Committee
a body that buys things on behalf of the US government
how the hell did you pull something like that?
how did you manage to organise that?
dirty politicians
corrupt politicians
to play hardball
to operate in a ruthless way

PARTING SHOTS   Here are six things that you might say at the end of a conversation.

1 Find six phrases in the film script with similar meanings. Which of the phrases is unfriendly?

a Have a nice meal. _____

b I'm not going to listen to any more. _____

c All the best. _____

d I'm afraid I have to go outside. _____

e It was nice meeting you. _____

f Excuse me, I have to find my friend. _____

2 Add any other phrases with similar meanings that you can think of.

APOLOGISING   **1** Here are three ways of apologising ... Match them with the appropriate situation.

APOLOGY	SITUATION
1 I beg your pardon.	*a* You want someone to move out of the way.
2 I'm sorry.	*b* You've bumped into someone.
3 Excuse me.	*c* You want someone to repeat what they've said.

2 You can also use two of the above phrases to apologise when you leave a social situation. Which are they?

SAYING GOODBYE   ... and here are six ways of saying goodbye. Again, match them with the appropriate situation.

PHRASE	SITUATION
1 Thank you for your attention, ladies and gentlemen.	*a* A chat with a friend.
2 See you. Take it easy.	*b* A business meeting.
3 It's been a pleasure doing business with you.	*c* A successful negotiation.
4 Let's call it a day.	*d* An unsuccessful interview.
5 Don't call us, we'll call you.	*e* A business trip.
6 Have a good journey.	*f* A presentation.

LEAVING ROLES   Use phrases from the script and others that you know in these situations.

▌ You are in the middle of a business lunch, when suddenly you feel ill and have to leave the room. What do you say to the other people at the table?

▌ On a business trip abroad, you have to leave a party early because you have an early flight the next morning. What do you say to your host?

▌ After a few minutes' conversation with someone at a reception, you are bored. How do you finish the conversation?

interactions

1 connections

focus *Culture and communication*

A CULTURE QUESTIONNAIRE

Q.1 Percentage of people who do <u>not</u> show emotions at work:

Italy 29%	UK 71%
France 34%	Japan 83%
USA 40%	

Q.2 Percentage of people who say that respect does <u>not</u> depend on family background:

Russia 53%	UK 76%
Italy 64%	USA 77%
Germany* 65%	

* This figure is for the former West Germany.

Q.3 Percentage of people who think that the individual should take responsibility:

Austria 28%	Spain 47%
Japan 36%	Russia 68%
USA 40%	

Q.4 Percentage of people who think that a good manager allows people to work alone:

China 57%	USA 83%
Japan 71%	France 89%
Italy 78%	

Q.5 Percentage of people who would <u>not</u> help the boss with his house-painting:

China 28%	USA 89%
Austria 65%	UK 92%
Spain 71%	

[Source: *Riding The Waves of Culture*, Fons Trompenaars]

2 the company

focus *Hanson*

HANSON'S EMPIRE

James Hanson decided to divide his companies up in the following way:

1 **Millennium Chemicals**
   Includes: SCM, Quantum

2 **Energy**
   Includes: Peabody, Eastern

3 **Imperial Tobacco**

4 **New Hanson**
   Includes: ARC, Cornerstone, Hanson Brick

NB There are no right and wrong answers to this case study. Many businesspeople think that these groups will change dramatically over the next few years.

3 money

doing **business 1** *Figures*

ACCOUNTING ROLES

BALANCE SHEET AT MARCH 31	£
FIXED ASSETS	....30,000....
Land	20,000
Buildings	50,000
CURRENT ASSETS	....35,000....
Stock	....10,000....
Debtors	5,000
Cash	50,000
CREDITORS (falling due within 12 months)	....90,000....
	(40,000)
NET CURRENT LIABILITIES	
TOTAL ASSETS LESS CURRENT LIABILITIES	....10,000....
CAPITAL	....10,000....

PROFIT AND LOSS ACCOUNT FOR THE YEAR TO MARCH 31

	This year	Last year
TURNOVER	200,000	...240,000...
Cost of sales	..160,000....	180,000
Gross profit	....40,000....	60,000
Administration costs	15,000	......20,000...
OPERATING PROFIT	....25,000....	40,000

6 the **customer**

doing **business 2** *Negotiating roles*

THE ANTIQUE STALL NEGOTIATION

A (**the buyer**): You have a maximum of £150 to spend, but don't really want to spend more than £100. You would love to get the picture, but you also want to buy three presents for your family.

▌ *For B's solution, see next page* ▌

focus *Four negotiating problems*

WHAT'S YOUR BEST PRICE?

Gavin Kennedy says ...

a He eats people like you for breakfast! His intimidation has worked and he knows what you can do.

b If you concede at your first meeting, what will you do at a longer meeting in six months' time?

c A bit better: but this is still not your best move.

d Yes. Tell him to call you when he gets back and say that you will talk to his technical people about exactly what they need. After all, they may desperately want your parts and he can worry about that all the way to Australia – and back!

GOING ROUND IN CIRCLES

Gavin Kennedy says ...

a With the Japanese, you could wait a long time!

b Concessions like these just encourage the other person to sit and wait for the next free gift.

c Yes. The Japanese will get the message.

d Weak. It shows your impatience.

DAMAGED GOODS

Gavin Kennedy says ...

a Only do this if you think you can get a discount for the non-damaged copy.

b This gives you a case for a discount.

c Yes. Evidence always helps to get a price reduction. If they still say no, leave both copies at the desk and go to another bookshop.

A SHARPLY-DRESSED MAN

Gavin Kennedy says ...

a A strange choice!

b You've been intimidated.

c Yes. Don't judge status by clothes.

[Source: *Everything is Negotiable*, Gavin Kennedy]

social skills   *Restaurants*

MENUS

RESTAURANT MENU

Arthur Gruffy's

STARTERS
Asparagus soup
Stuffed mushrooms
Waldorf salad

POULTRY
Chicken breast with tomatoes and cheese
Duckling in orange sauce
Roast pheasant

MEAT
Fillet steak in brandy (cooked at the table)
Roast pork
Lamb stew

FISH
Fresh lobster
Grilled salmon in sauce
Grilled trout with almonds

PUDDINGS
Ice cream (imported from the USA!)
A selection of fruit from the trolley

All our main dishes come with choice of salad
or a selection of fresh vegetables

doing **business 2** *Negotiating roles*

THE ANTIQUE STALL NEGOTIATION

B **(the owner of the stall)**: You have had a bad day and really need to make some more money today. All the antiques are on sale for twice the price that you paid for them.

8 **business** and **society**.

Economic VOCABULARY

WHO SAID THAT?

1 Clinton *2* Mandela *3* Havel *4* Blair

social skills Parties!

BONFIRE ROLES

What Sherman actually said (he did the best he could) was: 'Would you do me a great favor? What is the name of the gentleman to my right, the thin gentleman?'

The Bonfire of the Vanities, Tom Wolfe

9 **business ethics**

GRAMMAR REVIEW

THREE MORE BUSINESS PROBLEMS

When Elias Howe discovered that Singer had stolen his patent, he took him to court and, after a lengthy legal battle, Singer agreed to pay Howe a royalty on every machine that was built. Strangely, rather than enjoying his new wealth, Elias Howe then went off to enlist in the Union Army as an ordinary foot soldier.

In response to pressure from the Coke-drinking public, less than 90 days after the launch of New Coke, old style Coca-Cola was re-introduced to the market under the name 'Classic Coke'.

Benzene (the substance found in Perrier water in 1990) is an industrial solvent and carcinogen, but the amount detected in Perrier was far too low to be any danger. The problem, that workers had failed to replace a filter at Perrier's spring, was soon rectified. However, the company realised that it needed to take dramatic action to safeguard its image, so it withdrew of every bottle of Perrier in circulation (all 160 million of them) and simply poured the water away. The total cost to the company was estimated at around $200 million.

focus *Levi Strauss & Co.*

LEVI'S AND CHILD LABOUR

What Levi's did was to work out a compromise with the contractors: if they continued to pay wages and agreed to hire the children back when they reached 14, Levi's would pay for school uniforms, books and tuition. The deal sounds expensive all around. But, between the two of them, Levi's and its contractor have spent just a few thousand dollars.

[Source: *Business Week*, September 12, 1994]

LEVI'S AND THE FACTORY CLOSURE

What Levi's did was to make generous payments to all the workers at the San Antonio factory, pay for extra education and training and help them find new jobs. But many former workers still complained that Levi's had not acted fairly.

[Source: *The Frontiers of Excellence*, Robert Waterman]

10 the **digital revolution**

Hi-tech VOCABULARY

'Anyone who has followed my work knows that I'm no fan of organization charts. I think they're a waste of even recycled paper. I recently ran across ... a Jackson Pollock painting which to me looks the way a corporate organization chart should look like. It's a depiction of ... a total intertwining of people without regard to rank or function or location.'

[Source: *The Tom Peters Seminar*, Macmillan]

doing **business 2** *e-mail 2*

EDITING ACTIVITY

Dear Mr Adebayo,

Your colleague, Jane Rodber, told me that you are now ready to consider our proposal. Of course, I'm delighted to hear this news. However, I am on vacation for the next four days and so won't be able to deal personally with any queries until I get back.

My secretary will call you to arrange a meeting after my return when I hope we can discuss the matter further.

I look forward to meeting you,

With best wishes,

Brian de Glanville

Contents

1 Articles

a/an, the and zero article

Uses of *a/an*

1 Before unspecified singular countable nouns:
*If you start **a** business you may need **a** loan.*
*She works for **an** international organisation.*
*He's bought **a** new Rolls Royce.*

2 Before the names of professions:
*John Baker is **a** lawyer. His wife is **an** accountant.*

3 In expressions of measurement:
*The fund produces a return of 35% **a** year.*
*Their minimum wage is about £5 **an** hour.*

Uses of *the*

1 Before a specific noun that we have mentioned before:
*I bought a computer and a modem but took **the** modem back because it was defective.*

2 When it is clear what particular thing or place we are referring to:
***The** photocopier isn't working.*
*I'll meet you in **the** lobby at **the** hotel.*

3 Before adjectives to specify a category of people or things:
***the** unemployed   **the** rich   **the** public*
*Business couldn't be done without **the** telephone.*

4 Before some institutions:
***the** World Bank   **the** United Nations*
***the** Stock Exchange   **the** IMF*

5 In superlative expressions
*Intel is **the** biggest producer of microchips.*

Uses of zero article

We use **no article (zero article)**:

1 Before nouns used with a general meaning:
Time is money.
Profit today isn't necessarily profit tomorrow.
Managers should be good leaders.

2 Before the names of most countries, cities, roads and people:
My boss, Dr. Foster, lives in Station Road, Canterbury and has a holiday home in Scotland.

PRACTICE

1 Fill in the blanks with *a, an, the* or Ø (zero article) .

  1 _____ money makes _____ world go around.
     Internet access costs about $10 _____ month.

  2 I'll meet you in _____ reception area.

  3 She goes skiing at least twice _____ year.

  4 You can find all _____ information you need on our web site.

  5 She always wanted to be _____ engineer in _____ multinational corporation.

  6 He's worked at _____ Stock Exchange ever since he left his job in _____ insurance.

  7 _____ politics is said to be _____ art of _____ possible.

  8 We're exporting more to _____ China and _____ Pacific Rim.

  9 The new left-wing government wants to transfer _____ wealth from _____ rich to _____ poor.

 10 He's got two cars: _____ Volvo and _____ Porsche but he doesn't drive _____ Porsche to _____ work.

2 Complete the following extract with *the* or Ø article.

There is only one meeting place in [1] _____ Africa like this. Lying in [2] _____ heart of [3] _____ Ethiopian capital, [4] _____ Addis Ababa, [5] _____ new United Nations Conference Centre (UNCC-AA) combines [6] _____ architectural elegance with [7] _____ very latest technology to offer [8] _____ ideal venue for [9] _____ meetings of all [10] _____ kinds.

Here, in a fully integrated complex under one roof, [11] _____ conference planners will find [12] _____ environment to ensure their aims are achieved with [13] _____ greatest of success.

From welcoming [14] _____ government delegates to facilitating [15] _____ press, from staging [16] _____ exhibitions to hosting [17] _____ dinners, UNCC-AA meets every need efficiently and professionally, a promise backed by more than 40 years' experience.

2 Comparisons

comparative and superlative adjectives; comparisons with *whereas + while*

1 To make comparisons we add *-er* to adjectives of one syllable. We form the superlative by adding *-est*.
*I've never worked har**der** in all my life.*
*Tokyo is Japan's larg**est** city.*

2 The majority of two-syllable adjectives, all longer adjectives, and adverbs ending in *-ly* use *more/less* for the comparative and *most/least* for the superlative.
*The new packaging is **more** attractive **than** the old one.*
*Lisbon is **less** expensive **than** London.*
*Please drive **more** carefully.*
*I think Venice is **the most** beautiful city in the world and Pittsburgh is **the least**.*
*The take-over affected our firm **most** seriously.*

3 After a comparative adjective or adverb, we often use *than*.
*Tokyo is larg**er than** Hong Kong.*
*For me Monday is **less** convenient **than** Friday.*
*When the crash came, it happened **more** dramatically **than** anyone had expected.*

4 We also use comparative and superlative adjectives in front of a noun.
*Self-employed people often sell their services to **more than** one organisation.*
*McDonald's has hamburger restaurants in **more than** 100 countries serving **more than** 30 million people a day.*
*Warren Buffet has a personal fortune of **more than** $8.5 bn and is one of the richest men in the world.*

5 When we want to say that one situation depends on another, we can make a 'parallel comparison'.
***The bigger** an organisation is, **the more difficult** its administration becomes.*
***The wider** investors spread their bets, **the less risky** their portfolios are.*

6 It is possible to link comparatives with *and*.
*Goods are getting **more and more** expensive.*
*Our firm is doing **better and better**.*

7 We use *as ... as* to compare people or things that are similar or identical.
*They're just **as** competitive **as** we are.*
*We're doing **as** well **as** we did last year.*

8 We can use the words *whereas* or *while* to make a contrast.
*I believe in spending more **whereas** he wants to make economies.*

PRACTICE

1 European companies trading within the EU can recover value added tax on certain categories of expenditure. But it may take time!

Look at the table below and make comparisons using these adjectives:
fast   slow   high   low   long

COUNTRY	NAME OF TAX	RATE	AVERAGE DELAY (months)
Sweden	MOMS	25%	3
Finland	ALV	22%	6
Ireland	VAT	21%	4
Italy	IVA	19%	24
Luxembourg	BTW	15%	18

1 Sweden has the _____ rate.
2 Luxembourg has the _____ rate.
3 The rate in Italy is _____ in Ireland.
4 The rate in Finland is _____ in Ireland.
5 The rate in Finland is not _____ in Sweden.
6 It takes _____ to get a refund from Finland _____ from Sweden.
7 Recovery of VAT is _____ from Sweden and _____ from Italy.

2 Rewrite the sentences using a superlative, as in the example.

I had never been to such a boring meeting.
It was the most boring meeting I had ever been to.

1 I'd never made such an unsuccessful deal.
2 I'd never paid so much for a meal before.
3 I've never read such a confusing set of instructions.
4 The chemicals division was not as profitable as any of the other divisions.

3 Make parallel comparisons as in the example, using these prompts.

He speaks fast → it is difficult to understand.
The faster he speaks, the more difficult it is to understand.

1 we leave soon → we arrive early
2 people wait long → people become impatient
3 I get old → I feel young!
4 you work hard → the rewards are high

3 Conditionals

0, 1, 2, 3

We use *if* to talk about a situation that might possibly happen and to say what its results could be.

1 When we talk about something that is generally true or often happens, we use the present simple or present perfect tense in the main clause and the present simple in the conditional clause.

If *you press this button, you* **get** *coffee with sugar.*
They usually **tell** *the accountant* **if** *they have overspent.*

2 It is also possible to use an imperative or a modal verb in the main clause.

Give *me a ring* **if** *anything* **goes** *wrong.*
They **must** *change their product range* **if** *they* **want** *to survive.*

3 To talk about something that may happen in the future, we use *will* in the main clause.

If *you go to Tehran, you* **will** *need a visa.*
If *I see her today, I'll give her your report.*

4 *If ... not* and *unless* have a similar meaning. Compare:

You cannot dine in the club **if** *you do***n't** *have a membership card.*
You cannot dine in the club **unless** *you have a membership card.*

5 When we talk about something we think is impossible or unlikely to happen, we use the past simple or past continuous in the conditional clause and *would* in the main clause.

If *I knew the answer, I* **would** *tell you.*
If *he was coming, he* **would** *ring.*

6 When we talk about things that did not happen and imagine how things might have been different in the past we use

if + past perfect + would/could/might + have + past participle.

If *he* **had had** *more experience, we* **could have given** *him the job.*
What **would** *you* **have done if** *you* **had been** *on the management team?*

7 *Were* is sometimes used instead of *was* in the conditional clause.

If *the world* **were** *run by economists, would it be a better place?*
If *I* **were** *you, I'd take proper advice.*
If *he* **were** *CEO, he'd downsize.*

PRACTICE

1 Match the two halves of these sentences.

1 If you send a parcel by UPS,
2 If you use a freephone number,
3 If a firm does not invest in R and D,
4 If income tax rates go down,
5 If you pay in cash,
6 If payment has already been made,

a British exporters find it more difficult to sell abroad.
b please disregard this letter.
c you don't have to pay for the call.
d it arrives the following morning.
e its products rapidly become obsolete.
f you get a 10% discount.

2 Rewrite these sentences using a first conditional sentence with *if*.

Send $100 today and get your free gift by return.
If you send $100 today, you'll get your free gift by return.

1 Unless payment is made by the end of the month, we will be forced to take legal action.
2 Defective items will be exchanged on production of a receipt.
3 You can learn more about our products by consulting our website http://www.gbpro.co.uk.
4 Your audience won't hear you unless you speak clearly.

3 Write sentences to say what you would do in these imaginary situations.

1 work in Beijing → learn Chinese
2 take a cut in salary → work fewer hours
3 have more time → take up golf
4 win the national lottery → retire

4 Write a sentence beginning with *if* for each of the following situations.

1 I didn't know the post was vacant so I didn't apply.
2 I missed my flight because there was a road accident.
3 I didn't get in touch with you because my mobile phone wasn't working.
4 He wasn't insured so he had to pay for his medical expenses himself.

4 Countable and uncountable nouns (1)

Countable nouns include:

individual things, people and places:
a building, *a computer*, *a manager*, *an office*, *a report*

units of measurement:
a metre, *a mile*, *a pound*, *a gallon*, *a kilo*

Countable nouns:
- can be used in the plural
- follow words such as *many*, *these*, *those*, *several*, *few*, *a few*
- are used with *a/an*

Uncountable nouns include:

substances:
gas, *gold*, *plastic*, *water*

many abstract ideas:
profitability, *progress*, *safety*, *travel*, *weather*

verbal nouns: *brainstorming*, *engineering*, *job-sharing*, *timing*, *video-conferencing*

Uncountable nouns
- take the singular form of the verb
- have words like *much*, *a little*, *little*, *some* before them
- do not take *the* when used in a general sense

Some of the more common uncountable nouns are:

accommodation	advertising	advice	baggage
cash	damage	employment	equipment
furniture	information	insurance	legislation
luggage	merchandise	money	news	progress
research	software	transport	traffic	travel
weather	work		

Countable and **uncountable** are grammatical terms. For example, although it is perfectly possible to count 'money' the word is grammatically uncountable. Therefore it is not possible to say 'a money' or 'two monies'.

PRACTICE

1 Cross out the incorrect alternative in the following sentences.

1 I've ordered *a/some* new software.

2 I have *a/some* good news for you.

3 I need *an/some* information about visas.

4 We've made *a/some* progress since we met.

5 The fire didn't cause *much/many* damage.

6 They say that *the/Ø* travel broadens the mind.

7 She never uses public *transport/transports*.

8 There was *a heavy/some heavy* traffic this morning.

9 We've done *a little/a few* research into the causes of the problem.

10 I was given *another/some more* training when I started my present job.

2 Find five pairs of words with similar or related meanings in the list below. One of each pair must be countable and the other uncountable. Write them in the appropriate columns as in the example.

~~suitcase~~   legislation   law   cash   ~~luggage~~   meal   coin   advert   catering   advertising

COUNTABLE	UNCOUNTABLE
suitcase	luggage

3 Complete the dialogues, using an appropriate noun in each case.

1 Was it difficult to find _____ ?
No, I found a nice flat overlooking the river.

2 Have they done much _____ into new uses for radioactive material?
Yes, they did some interesting experiments last year.

3 Did she give you any _____ ?
Yes, she made a very good suggestion.

4 Did you find _____ easily?
No, it was difficult to find a suitable job.

1 Many nouns have both countable **C** and uncountable **U** uses. For example:

There was **a time** when all our products were made in the UK. **C**
We have very little **time** left. **U**

Waiter, there's **a hair** in my soup. **C**
He has short red **hair**. **U**

The director has put up **a notice** on the bulletin board. **C**
He's been given **notice** of dismissal. **U**

The court awarded $1 million in **damages**. **C**
The insurance company estimated the **damage** at £850 000. **U**

He gave **a talk** at the annual conference. **C**
Be careful of what you say; **talk** is cheap round here. **U**

2 Some uncountable nouns (*travel; work*) have a countable equivalent which is a completely different word (*trip/journey; job/task; advice/suggestion*).

Business **travel** is a big industry. **U**
I'm going on a business **trip** to Beijing. **C**
The **journey** from Paris to Geneva took five hours. **C**

I've got a lot of **work** to do. **U**
Each section head is responsible for a particular **job/task**. **C**

She gave me some good **advice**. **U**
One **suggestion** she made was excellent. **C**

3 There are nouns which only occur in the plural. For example:
The **goods** are being sent by air freight.
Earnings per share have risen slightly.
We've opened new **premises** in Rio.
Could you pass me the **scissors**?
Don't leave **valuables** in your car.

4 We can refer to parts of a mass by using a suitable singular expression in front of the noun.
a **piece** of advice, a **piece** of equipment, a **sheet** of paper, a **show** of strength, a **spell** of bad weather, a **pair** of scissors

PRACTICE

1 Decide what is wrong in the following sentences. Make the necessary corrections.

1 She's slim, quite tall, attractive and has black hairs.
2 She's received a notice to quit the firm by the end of the month.
3 I need a scissor to cut out the article.
4 A paper is made of wood.
5 Did you have a good travel to Tokyo?
6 A light travels at 186,000 miles a second.
7 The equipment is made of an iron and a reinforced glass.

2 Match the words in box A with those in box B.

A	B
a bottle of	inspiration
a barrel of	work
a stroke of	applause
a pair of	oil
a flash of	perfume
a mountain of	luck
a round of	jeans

3 Use the expressions in Exercise 2 appropriately in the following sentences.

1 The solution to the problem came to him in a _____ .
2 He made a passionate speech and got a huge _____ .
3 He bought a _____ for his wife from the duty-free.
4 He surprised everybody by coming to work wearing a _____ .
5 OPEC has fixed the price of a _____ at $19.
6 Please don't disturb me under any circumstances. I've got a _____ to get through.
7 I had a _____ at the airport – they gave me an earlier flight and an upgrade to a first-class cabin.

6 *Future forms*

1 To make a prediction about the future, we can use either *will* or *going to*.
*I'm sure you **will/are going to** enjoy your visit to our Head Office.*

When we talk about present intentions for the future we use *going to* rather than *will*.
*She is **going to** retire in two years' time.*

2 When making a promise or an offer, we use *will*, often contracted to *'ll*, when the decision has just been made.
I'll get the report to you by tomorrow.
I'll give you a lift to the airport if you like.

3 To talk about plans or future arrangements, we use either the present continuous or the future continuous.
I'm meeting Mr Wong next week.
During your internship, you'll be learning about negotiation strategies.

4 For a future event based on an official calendar or schedule, we use the present simple. The event is unlikely to change between now and then.
*The train **leaves** from Waterloo at 10.59.*
*Our next planning meeting **is** on Wednesday.*

5 For events that will be completed before a time in the future, we use the future perfect simple.
*By the time she arrives we **will have finished**.*

If the event is still in progress, we use the continuous form.
This time next year I'll be lying on the beach in Malibu.

6 If a condition has to be met before something can happen, we use the present perfect to refer to the future event.
*We won't start until everyone **has arrived**.*
I'll e-mail you when I've made all the arrangements.

7 In time clauses, we use the present simple to refer to the future. It is incorrect to use *will* in a time clause.
*Please get in touch when you **know** her answer.*
*We won't start until everyone **arrives**.*
*Switch off the computer before you **leave**.*
*As soon as I **get** home, I'll pour myself a gimlet.*

PRACTICE

1 Decide which of these sentence pairs is grammatically correct. Cross out the sentence which is wrong.

1 I'm going to give you a lift if you like.
I'll give you a lift if you like.

2 The agreement will have expired by the end of the month.
The agreement will have been expiring by the end of the month.

3 She says she's not going to apply for the vacancy.
She says she doesn't apply for the vacancy.

4 I'll phone you as soon as I will know the price.
I'll phone you as soon as I know the price.

5 During the course you'll be improving your communication skills.
During the course you'll have improved your communication skills.

2 Mr Baxter is visiting Germany next week. Describe his schedule for each day of the week.

	AM	PM
Mon.	BA436 – Berlin dep. 16.35 arr 18.05	check into Regency Hotel
Tue.	meet Herr Eicher	visit agent's premises
Wed.	present 1st quarter sales results	attend seminar on 'Selling in E. Europe'
Thurs.	drive to Potsdam – tour of new offices	lunch with Frau Grabe (13.00)
Fri.	LH529 – Heathrow dep 10.05 arr 11.35	off

3 Make predictions using either the future continuous or the future perfect.

1 In a few years' time many more employees (work) from home.

2 Over the next ten years voice telephony over the Internet (increase) rapidly.

3 By 2010 most European textile firms (go bankrupt).

4 By 2025 paper money (disappear).

5 By 2050 75% of businesspeople (use) Chinese for their commercial transactions.

6 By the end of the 21st century small, family aircraft (replace) privately-owned cars.

7 *Linking words*

To help people to understand a written or spoken message clearly, we use linking words to connect one idea to another. These words and phrases are like signposts, making it easier for the reader or listener to understand. Linking words have several functions:

1 Ordering and sequencing:

before	at the same time	then	earlier
simultaneously	next	previously	meanwhile
subsequently	first (of all)	in the meantime	
afterwards	finally/in the end/lastly		

First we did our market research, **then** looked for an agent. **Next** we ran a promotional campaign but **in the meantime** we found out our competitors had got there **beforehand** and **subsequently** we decided to concentrate on another region.

2 Making a contrast:

although	conversely	nevertheless	alternatively
even so	on the other hand	by contrast	however

The government may try to increase the rate of income tax. **Alternatively**, it could put up VAT.
Although some people condemn industrial espionage, it is **nevertheless** a fact of life.
Last year we made a large profit. **However**, we are operating in an unstable market and results may not be so good next year.

3 Indicating cause and effect:

as a result	so	consequently	therefore

CAUSE	EFFECT
The machine was damaged and,	**as a result**, the assembly line had to be shut down.

CAUSE	EFFECT
There was a lot of fog at the airport	**so** the plane couldn't take off.

4 Indicating a change in topic:

anyhow	by the way	anyway	incidentally

Oh, **by the way**, have you heard that Derek has decided to resign?
Anyway, as I was saying earlier, quality control is the key to success.

5 Correcting a statement that is the opposite of what people would expect:

actually	as it happens	as a matter of fact	in fact

Actually, I do know why he changed his mind.

PRACTICE

1 Choose the best alternative in each case to complete the sentences.

1 _____ we've been doing well, we must remain vigilant.
(*a*) In the meantime   (*b*) Although   (*c*) However

2 Some people say they want a good job – _____ , they're not prepared to work hard to get it.
(*a*) consequently   (*b*) then   (*c*) on the other hand

3 The firm was facing a cash flow crisis. _____ , it had to borrow money from the bank.
(*a*) As a result   (*b*) Earlier   (*c*) By the way

4 We thought we were only going to stay in the area for a year but _____ we ended up staying for ten years.
(*a*) conversely   (*b*) as a result   (*c*) actually

2 Complete the following section from a report using these words.

at the same time   first of all   so   in conclusion
secondly

There are many reasons for the decline. [1]_____ , the quality of management has been uninspired. [2]_____ , output has not kept up with demand. Failure to identify suitable markets has, [3]_____ , meant that demand has peaked, [4]_____ saturation point will be reached very quickly. [5]_____ , unless there are radical changes, future prospects are not encouraging.

3 Complete the memo using these words.

however   although   nevertheless   alternatively
therefore   as a result   on the contrary

MEMO

[1]_____ we have agreed in principle to reduce staffing levels, there is [2]_____ a problem in my own section. Mrs Baxter, who works in reception during the morning, is also in charge of reprography. [3]_____ , there are times when senior staff members are having to make their own photocopies which means they are wasting valuable time doing routine tasks.

I [4]_____ suggest we take on a part-time receptionist. [5]_____ , we could take up Bill's suggestion and ask Mrs Davies, who is shortly to return from maternity leave, to work in reception during the morning. [6]_____ , this would not, in my opinion, be a satisfactory solution. [7]_____ , it would create a certain amount of disruption elsewhere.

8 Must *and* have to

1 We use *must* and *has/have to* to indicate what is compulsory in the present and future.
   *A senior manager often **has to** make tough decisions.*
   *The longer people **have to** wait, the more impatient they become.*
   *In order to make its products known, a firm **must** advertise.*
   *All tenders **must** be submitted by 31 March.*

2 We prefer to use *must* when we impose the obligation on ourselves. We prefer *have to* when the obligation is imposed by other people or external circumstances.
   *I **must** remember to send a fax to Mr Warner; I keep forgetting.*
   *We **have to** wear a badge at work; it's a rule.*
   *I enjoy going to conferences unless I **have to** make a speech.*

3 If you *do not have to* do something, there is no obligation – you can do it if you want to.
   *I can work from home so I **don't have to** go into the office very often.*

   Do not confuse *not have to* with *must not*. We use *must not* to say that something is forbidden or unacceptable.
   *Passengers **must not** smoke during take-off.*
   *You **mustn't** sign the contract on those terms.*

4 If something was necessary or obligatory in the past, we use *had to*.
   *When we lived in Tokyo we **had to** learn some Japanese.*

5 If we want to say that an action is obligatory in the future, we use *will have to*.
   *We **will have to** monitor progress carefully.*

   The absence of obligation is expressed by *will not/won't have to*.
   *With this employment protection policy, you **won't have to** worry about losing your job.*

6 *Must* is used to make deductions about the present and *must have* is used for past circumstances.
   *It **must** be difficult to have five young children, a husband and a top job in the City.*
   *In 1995, Nick Leeson **must have** been a very worried man.*

   If you infer that something is untrue, you use *cannot*.
   *Sell at a loss! You **can't** be serious!*
   *He **can't have** been at that meeting – he was 2,000 miles away.*

PRACTICE

1 Complete the following travel information using *must*, *have to*, *must not* and *do not have to*.

🌐 **PASSPORTS AND VISAS**

All travellers [1]_____ hold a valid passport. For certain destinations, you [2]_____ have a full 10-year passport and not simply a 1-year visitor's passport. For many countries, you [3]_____ also apply for a visa.

🌐 **HEALTH REGULATIONS**

For certain countries, you [4]_____ be vaccinated against cholera and yellow fever and other tropical diseases.

🌐 **INSURANCE**

Although you [5]_____ take out extra cover, you may want to think about insuring yourself against unexpected medical expenses or loss of baggage and personal possessions.

🌐 **FLIGHT DEPARTURES**

Passengers [6]_____ check in an hour before departure. Remember that you are allowed to take one piece of hand luggage on board but it [7]_____ measure more than 55 × 40 × 20 cm.

🌐 **CUSTOMS**

Please check which goods are eligible for duty before you pass through customs. You [8]_____ attempt to enter with firearms, drugs or narcotics.

2 How would you interpret these signs? Use *must*, *have to*, *don't have to* and *must not*.

3 Cross out the inappropriate alternative in the following sentences.

1 It's my wife's birthday! I really *must/have to* remember to get her a present.

2 All visitors *must/have to* report to the reception area and obtain a badge.

3 Unfortunately, he *must/has to* wear a hearing aid – he's a bit deaf in one ear.

4 You *must/have to* visit us again, it's been a real pleasure.

9 *Nouns in groups*

apostrophe *s* (*'s*)

1 We use *'s* to express a relationship between a person or animal and another person, animal or thing.
Peter's friends   *his wife's job*   *the lion's share*

2 *'s* can be used to show that something belongs to or is associated with a group of people, a place or an organisation.
the board's decision   Singapore's success
New York's Fifth Avenue   our company's policy
the bank's corporate clients

3 *'s* is used with nouns referring to the duration of an event or a specific time.
a week's holiday   yesterday's newspaper
at a moment's notice   a day's work

4 *'s* is added to a noun that specifies a part of an object or a quality it has.
the computer's memory   the car's design

Compound nouns

These are commonly formed by placing two or three nouns together. The first noun classifies the second.
an assembly line   a credit card   a bank account
a parking meter   an air traffic controller
a sales training seminar

When compound nouns are used in expressions of measurement with a numeral, the first noun is singular.
a fifty-dollar bill   a five-day course

of

1 We tend to combine two nouns with *of* when referring to more abstract concepts.
the history of business   the meaning of life

2 With words that indicate a part of something, we use this *of* structure:
the end of the meeting   the top of the page
the front of the building   the moment of truth

3 We also prefer the *of* structure with words that refer to units or a certain quantity of something.
an article of clothing   an ounce of gold
a round of negotiations   a stroke of luck

PRACTICE

1 Only one of the following *a*, *b*, or *c* is an acceptable noun combination. Choose the correct one.

1 *a* yesterday's paper
   b a paper of yesterday
   c yesterday paper

2 *a* a network of telephone
   b a telephone's network
   c a telephone network

3 *a* a bonus scheme
   b a scheme of bonus
   c a scheme's bonus

4 *a* the book of Charles Handy
   b Charles Handy's book
   c the Charles Handy's book

5 *a* economies of scale
   b scale economies
   c scale's economies

6 *a* a bear market
   b a bear's market
   c a market of bears

2 Match the nouns in the two columns of box A. Then do the same with those in box B.

A		B	
market	spending	voice	limit
consumer	sheet	brand	costs
laser	forces	labour	stripper
balance	executive	asset	resort
service	printer	time	mail
chief	industry	ski	leader

3 Put the three words into the right order to make acceptable noun phrases.

1 programme training management
2 trade world centre
3 project generation power
4 rate exchange mechanism
5 control procedure quality
6 opportunity investment overseas
7 analysis questionnaire needs

10 Passive

1 We often choose a passive construction when we are not interested in who performs an action or it is not necessary to know.
*The company **was founded** in 1986.*
*A new extension **is being built**.*

2 If we want to mention the person who performs the action, we can use a phrase beginning with *by*.
*The report **was written** by Mr Reed.*

In this sentence, the focus of attention is on the report; if we were more interested in the writer, we would choose an active construction.
Mr Reed wrote the report.

3 The passive is very often used when we describe a process or a procedure because we are less concerned with who has done something than in what is done.
*Applicants **are short-listed** and **interviewed**. The best candidate **is** then **offered** the job.*
*The manufacture of components **is sub-contracted** to outside suppliers.*

4 Changes of state and completed actions are described using the present perfect passive.
*She **has been promoted** to the post of Regional Sales Director.*
*The department **has been reorganised**.*
*The meeting **has been cancelled**.*

5 When writing in a formal style (e.g. reports/minutes), we often choose an impersonal style by using the passive and beginning sentences with *It*.
***It was felt** that some cuts had to be made.*
***It was decided** that the package design would be changed.*

6 Passive structures beginning with someone's name or a personal pronoun are followed by an object and infinitive.
*I **was asked** to send you a copy of the programme.*
*He **has been told** not to come back.*
*Mrs Fry **will be asked** to chair the meeting.*

PRACTICE

1 Match the two halves of these sentences.

1 A detailed conference programme
2 Please make sure that your portable telephone
3 All tenders and supporting documents
4 Please wait, your transaction
5 As requested, the sum of $19,500
6 It has to be admitted that

a structural unemployment cannot easily be solved.
b has been transferred to your off-shore account.
c will be sent to you on receipt of your fee.
d is switched off in this restaurant.
e should be returned by 31 March.
f is being processed.

2 Change the verbs in brackets into an appropriate active or passive form.

DAVID LEE (recognise)[1] world-wide as a leading scholar in the field of marketing. Since 1985, he (involve)[2] extensively with foreign companies doing business with China. Mr Lee (develop)[3] invaluable expertise in setting up and operating in the People's Republic. One of his latest articles 'Business in China: Managing Culture Shock' (publish)[4] in last month's issue of *Harvard Business Review*.

3 The following sentences are stages in the production and sale of a new model of car. Put them into the most logical order.

a The production tools and assembly lines are set up by the Process Engineering department.
b A prototype is built and tested for performance.
c The new model is distributed to dealers and sold to the public.
d The new model is built in selected factories.
e Each model is inspected by quality control personnel.
f The new model is developed by the Design and Product Planning department.
g The target market is predicted and defined by the Market Research department.
h The new model is launched to the press at official presentations.

Past continuous and past perfect simple v. continuous

The past continuous

1 We use the past continuous to say that something was in progress at and around a particular time in the past.
*He **was working** on the final report all night.*
*I **was trying** to get in touch with you all day yesterday.*

2 It can also be used for repeated actions.
*We got rid of the photocopier because it **was** always **breaking down**.*

3 The past continuous and past simple are often used together in a sentence; the past continuous describes a longer event which was interrupted by another.
*I **was** just **leaving** the building when he **arrived**.*
*My car **broke down** while I **was driving** from Milan to Rome.*

4 We sometimes use the past continuous to make a polite request.
*I **was wondering** if you could give me a lift back to the station.*

5 We use *was going to* to refer to events planned in the past, but which did not take place.
*I **was going to** phone her yesterday but I didn't find time.*

The past perfect

1 We use the past perfect to talk about an event that happened before a particular time in the past.
*Before I joined IBM, I **had had** seven other jobs.*
*By 1996, we **had sold** over two million copies.*

2 The past perfect can be used with *I wish, If only* and *I'd rather* to talk about events that did not happen.
*I wish she **had told** me about it earlier.*
*I'd rather she **had asked** me before taking my car.*

3 If we want to emphasise the recent nature and/or duration of continuous activity that took place in an earlier past, we use the continuous form.
*They **had been testing** the drug for years before it finally appeared on the market.*
*I was tired because I'**d been waiting** in the airport for hours.*

PRACTICE

1 Match the two halves of these sentences.

1 I couldn't show my slides
2 Her phone was disconnected
3 I couldn't access the file
4 The mail wasn't being delivered
5 The downtown area was closed to traffic
6 The satellite couldn't be launched
7 The cheque was refused

BECAUSE

a he had gone beyond his credit limit.
b the firm had changed address.
c an engineer had discovered a fuel leak.
d it had been corrupted by a virus.
e someone had stolen the overhead projector.
f a terrorist group had planted a bomb.
g she hadn't paid her bills.

2 Complete the passage using either the past simple, past continuous, past perfect simple or past perfect continuous. Sometimes more than one answer is possible.

On February 26 1995, the world (wake up)[1] to the news that Britain's oldest bank, Barings, (collapse)[2] because of the actions of just one man – a trader called Nick Leeson.

Leeson (start)[3] working at Barings' Singapore office in 1992, when he (be)[4] 25 years old. Using the bank's money, he (buy)[5] and (sell)[6] derivatives contracts on the Singapore Monetary Exchange. This can be a risky business, but Barings (think)[7] it (know)[8] what it (do)[9].

Leeson quickly (become)[10] the star of the Singapore office, and its profits from derivatives trading (be)[11] substantial. But in fact, he (hide)[12] even greater losses in a secret account.

The truth was that Nick Leeson (not behave)[13] like an ordinary trader. He (consider)[14] the financial markets as a gambling casino and, just like a losing gambler, he (believe)[15] that he would win in the end. So, towards the end of 1994, he (decide)[16] to solve his problems by making a very big gamble.

He (think)[17] that the Tokyo stock market would remain stable for the next few months. He (know)[18] that he could make a good profit by selling a special kind of option contract but, unfortunately for him, Japan (enter)[19] a very unstable period.

On 17 January 1995, a huge earthquake (hit)[20] the industrial city of Kobe. In response, the Tokyo stock market (plunge)[21]. Leeson's gamble (go)[22] badly wrong and by February 23, he (lose)[23] more than £300 million and the game was over. The following day, he and his wife (fly)[24] to Malaysia for a holiday.

12 *Past simple and present perfect*

Past simple

1 The past simple is used to talk about completed actions in the past.
Did *you check the figures?*
*Yes, and I **sent** them back to the purchasing department.*

2 The past simple is often used with expressions which refer to a definite moment or period in the past.
*He founded the business **20 years ago**.*
*The railways expanded **during the nineteenth century**.*
*I met her **yesterday**.*
*The exchange rate went up **in 1997**.*
*We **discussed** it at last week's meeting.*

The present perfect cannot be used in the above examples.
- ~~*He has founded the business 20 years ago.*~~
- ~~*I have met her yesterday.*~~
- ~~*We have discussed it at last week's meeting.*~~

3 We use the past simple after *I wish* and *If only* to talk about unfulfilled desires.
*I wish I **had** more time.*
*If only I **knew** how to get rich quickly.*

Present perfect

1 The present perfect connects both past and present time.
Have *you ever **visited** Thailand?*
*I've never **seen** the Taj Mahal.*
Have *you **decided** what to do yet?*
*She's **had** the same job for three years.*

2 We use the present perfect to say that a finished action in an unspecified past is relevant now.
*Our telephone number **has changed**.*
*We've **redesigned** our web site.*
*We **have updated** our prices.*

3 We use the present perfect to talk about recent events.
Here is the news for Monday, 26 July. The Prime Minister **has announced** *an increase in the tax on cigarettes. And we **have just learnt** that there **has been** an earthquake in Japan.*

4 We often use the present perfect to say how long a present situation has existed.
*We've **known** each other for twenty years.*
*He's **had** the same job since 1995.*
*He's always **been** a workaholic.*

P R A C T I C E

1 Match the two halves of these sentences.

1 National firms are finding it easier to export because
2 The workforce is smaller and more flexible because
3 Sales are now improving because
4 Ford wanted to expand into Eastern Europe so
5 The economy is badly in need of investment capital so

a the government has applied to the World Bank for a loan.
b we have started an aggressive advertising campaign.
c the Finance Minister has devalued the currency.
d it has opened an assembly plant in Belarus.
e they have made many employees redundant.

2 Complete the following dialogues, using the past simple or the present perfect.

A (You/ever/be)[1] to Cannes?
B Yes, I have. I (go)[2] for the film festival last year.
A Where (you/stay)[3]?
B We (book)[4] a room at the Carlton Hotel. It (be)[5] fabulous.
A (You/ever/make)[6] a presentation in English?
B Yes, I have. I (have to)[7] make one last month in fact.
A What (you/talk)[8] about?
B I (present)[9] our sales performance for the current year.

3 Complete the following passage, using either the past simple or the present perfect.

CHRISTIE HEFNER (be)[1] just one year old when her father, Hugh, (launch)[2] *Playboy* in 1963. In the early 70s, the magazine (sell)[3] more than 7m copies a month. But, by the 1980s, the business (be)[4] in decline and he (decide)[5] to make his daughter president. She (be)[6] the firm's chief executive since 1988.

Ms Hefner (become)[7] a case study on how to squeeze life from a tired brand without spending too much. She (reorganise)[8] the firm's finances and (get rid of)[9] its loss-making operations. She (take)[10] advantage of globalisation and technology. There are now over 15 overseas editions of *Playboy* and she (set up)[11] joint venture TV operations around the world.

Technologically, *Playboy* (become)[12] a leader. It (begin)[13] a few years ago to use digital satellite technology, a strategy that so far (proved)[14] a success because a larger proportion of satellite-TV viewers than cable-TV ones buy its programmes. It (be)[15] also the first big American magazine with a site on the World Wide Web. The result is that, last year, *Playboy* (make)[16] a $13.9m operating profit on its entertainment revenues, an increase of 276% on the year before.

13 *Present perfect simple and present perfect continuous*

1 Sometimes it is possible to use either the simple or continuous form with little or no change of meaning.

*London **has stood** on the banks of the Thames for hundreds of years.*

*London **has been standing** on the banks of the Thames for hundreds of years.*

*She's **lived** in Madrid since 1995.*

*She's **been living** in Madrid since 1995.*

2 At other times, the use of the simple implies that an action is complete and the continuous suggests that it is incomplete. For example:

(a) *We've **dealt** with your complaint.*

(b) *We've **been dealing** with your complaint.*

In (a) the implication is that there is nothing more to say or do. In (b) there is a suggestion that the matter is still being looked into.

Similarly:

(a) *He's **prepared** his presentation.* (it is finished)

(b) *He's **been preparing** his presentation.* (it may be finished, but there is an implication that he hasn't finished it yet)

(a) *She's **learnt** how to use the new spreadsheet.* (and can use it now)

(b) *She's **been learning** English for 10 years.* (this process is never complete!)

3 We use the continuous form to emphasise the duration of an event.

*So, ladies and gentlemen, what I **have been describing** is a crisis in our industry.*

4 We often use the continuous form to talk about the reasons for someone's present appearance.

*'You look tired.' 'Yes, I've **been running** around all day.'*

5 The present perfect continuous cannot be used with verbs describing states or beliefs, e.g. *believe, contain, know, realise, remember, understand, seem,* etc.

*I've **known** Mr Schmidt for years.*

(**NOT** ~~I've been knowing~~)

6 The continuous form is not used with *yet, still* and *already.*

***Has** he **left** yet?*

(**NOT** ~~Has he been leaving yet?~~)

*He's already **gone** home.*

(**NOT** ~~He's already been going home.~~)

PRACTICE

1 Complete the following letter appropriately.

Dear Sirs,

Please note that we (move)[1] to new premises in Paris and our address is now:
18 rue Saint Dominique
Paris 75350 Cedex 07

However, our telephone and fax numbers (not change)[2] and we (add)[3] a new line dedicated to after-sales service. This number is 00 33 1 44 77 11 99.

Monsieur Cuisinier is no longer sales manager for the Paris region and (move)[4] to our office in Brussels. We (appoint)[5] Mme. Douat as our new Paris region manager and she will be contacting you shortly.

I am enclosing a copy of our present catalogue. You will notice that, as the franc (fall)[6] all year against the dollar, the products we distribute for American firms (increase)[7] in price. However, these will be readjusted accordingly if and when the dollar falls.

We look forward to doing further business with you.

2 Match the two halves of these sentences.

1 They're still not fluent even though

2 They've been losing a lot of money

3 They've been selling up-market leather goods

4 They've been trying to get in touch

5 They've been talking about a merger

a to Harrods for over 25 years.

b but haven't agreed on the terms and conditions.

c because of the transport strike.

d they've been learning German for several years.

e while you've been away.

3 Complete the following fax, using either the present perfect simple or continuous.

Dear Leslie,

Sorry I (not be)[1] in touch sooner. I (mean)[2] to send you this fax for some time but I (be)[3] very busy since my arrival in Kowloon.

To cut a long story short, I (try)[4] to negotiate a deal with a local manufacturer of cigarette lighters. We (reach)[5] an agreement on 500,000 items at 8 pence each. They (guarantee)[6] to have the order ready for May 26.

I (do)[7] a lot of travelling over the last ten days but we still (not sign)[8] the most important contract. But I (made)[9] an appointment to see Peter Wu tomorrow and hope to finalise everything then.

14 Present simple and present continuous

Uses of the present simple

1 To talk about routines:
Mr Cheung **phones** *head office every day.*

2 To describe permanent situations and facts:
Unilever **makes** *a wide variety of household products.*
Low interest rates **discourage** *investment.*

3 With verbs of perception, possession, emotion and belief:
The coffee **tastes** *good.*
The firm **belongs to** *the Pearson group.*
She **detests** *inefficiency.*
I **believe** *in strong management.*

Other verbs in this category include:
appear, cost, doubt, involve, know, own, possess, prefer, recognise, regret, remember, seem, sound, understand, want, wish

Uses of the present continuous

1 To talk about an event at the moment of speaking:
I'm afraid Mrs Bell can't speak to you at the moment.
She's **talking** *to someone on the other line.*

2 To describe current situations and on-going projects:
I'm **dealing** *with your enquiry now.*
We're **designing** *a new advertising campaign.*

3 To describe temporary situations:
He's **staying** *at the Hyatt Regency Hotel until the end of next week.*
My car **is being** *repaired this week.*

4 To refer to changing, developing situations:
Some people feel the traditional company **is dying***.*

5 To talk about repeated actions:
His son **is taking** *driving lessons.*

(For more information about the use of present tenses to refer to future time, see page 133.)

PRACTICE

1 Make sentences about these organisations.

Benetton		chocolate and food products.
Yamaha		motor vehicles.
Indesit	makes	washing machines.
Compaq		motorbikes and musical instruments.
Nestlé		computers.
Fiat		clothing.

2 What do the graphs below portray? Use these verbs:
soar   plummet   grow   decline

1 Foreign direct investment

2 Profit margins

3 Unemployment levels

4 Union membership

3 Put the verbs into the present simple or the present continuous.

1 They (launch) a new product in Indonesia.
2 Good management (involve) both technical competence and people skills.
3 The new model (cost) $50,000.
4 We (regret) to inform you that your services are no longer required.
5 She (work) in a travel agency to get some practical experience.
6 Philips (manufacture) a wide range of consumer goods.
7 He (own) a 49% stake in the business.
8 They (perfect) a revolutionary computer game.
9 A laptop computer (enable) you to work on the plane as you (fly) to your next meeting.
10 Sorry, I'll be late for the meeting – I (sit) in a traffic jam on the M25.
11 I'm sorry about the noise. They (put in) a new central heating system.
12 The agency (try) to create a logo that (look) attractive.
13 We (organise) a market survey to find out what potential customers (require).
14 I (not understand) your comment. It (depend) on what you (mean) by 'effective'.

15 Quantifiers

When we want to talk about a number or amount of something we use quantifiers such as:

both   each   few   a few   little   a little
many   much

The choice of quantifier often depends on the kind of noun that follows it.

1   *Both* and *each* are used in front of plural noun groups.
    Both *(of the) documents have to be sent in triplicate.*
    (NOT ~~*the both documents*~~)
    Note that *each (of)* is followed by a singular verb form.
    Each *document **has** to be countersigned.*
    Each of *the documents **has** to be countersigned.*

2   *Few* means 'not many'. It is used before countable nouns and has a negative meaning.
    *If there are **few** opportunities for promotion, young high-flyers will look for another job.*
    Few *people like their boss interfering with their work.*

3   *A few* means 'some/a small number of'. It is used before countable nouns.
    *We'll all be doing our shopping by computer in **a few** years' time.*
    *You'll settle in after **a few** weeks.*

4   *Little* means 'not much' and is used with uncountable nouns. It is often preceded by 'very' and has a negative meaning.
    *There is **little** time left for discussion so we need to make a decision right away.*
    *There's **very little** space in my office.*

5   *A little* means 'a small amount' and is also used with uncountable nouns.
    *I need **a little** more time to think about your proposal.*
    *I like to mix business with **a little** pleasure.*

    It can also mean 'to some extent' when used with an adjective.
    *Profits were **a little** disappointing.*

6   We use *much* with uncountable nouns and singular noun groups. *Many* is used with plural nouns.
    *How **much** money have you got?*
    Much *of his day is spent doing paperwork.*
    *How **many** people work in your firm?*
    *We operate in **many** different countries.*

PRACTICE

1 Read these sentences. Put a tick (✓) next to the ones that are right and correct those that are wrong.

1   'Are there any seats left on the next flight to London?' 'Yes, but only a few.'

2   We've made a few progress but not many.

3   Each of the invoices have a different reference number.

4   There are two fools in any market: one asks too little, one asks too many.

5   Little expatriates want to live overseas for more than a few years.

6   The both candidates were excellent.

7   Research scientists spend too much time on administration and routine meetings.

8   How many times will it take you to finish?

9   There's very few data available about market trends in Myanmar.

10 Much of the money given in aid goes to the army.

2 Complete the memo appropriately using *few*, *a few*, *little* and *a little*.

MEMO

3RD QUARTER RESULTS

Sales were ¹_____ disappointing as very ²_____ stores are willing to stock and promote our goods. Their profit margin is low and there is consequently ³_____ incentive for them to display our products. However, sales have picked up ⁴_____ in the last two months or so.

⁵_____ customers (only 12%) feel that the design is attractive and sales have suffered as a consequence. However, artwork for a new design has been commissioned and ⁶_____ samples will be available for store buyers to look at.

However, we usually get ⁷_____ or no feedback from them and I'm beginning to get ⁸_____ worried about the situation in general.

16 Relative clauses

1 We use a relative clause beginning with *who* or *that* to identify a person or people.
  *Mr Lee was the person **who/that** set up the deal.*
  *The consultants **who/that** advised us were proved wrong.*

2 A relative clause beginning with *that* or *which* identifies a thing or things.
  *He's got a private yacht **that/which** he uses to entertain corporate clients.*
  *The equipment **that/which** we bought was expensive.*

3 If *who*, *which* or *that* is followed by a noun or pronoun + verb, we can leave it out.
  The spare parts Mr Spencer ordered have been delivered.
  He's the man I met in St Petersburg.

4 We use *whose* to indicate possession or a relationship. It can be used to refer to people or things.
  *He's the man **whose** wife has just been appointed Managing Director.*
  *In 1997, Michelin, **whose** tyre sales totalled $13.1bn, regained its position of market leader.*

5 *Where* is used to refer to places.
  *The village **where** we stayed was very pleasant.*

  If there is a preposition at the end of the clause, *where* is omitted.
  The village we stayed in was very pleasant.
  (**NOT** *The village ~~where~~ we stayed in …*)

  This can also be reformulated as:
  *The village **in which** we stayed was very pleasant.*

6 Relative clauses identify or define the previous noun or just add extra information.
  *The firm **that I work for** has a good pension scheme.*
    (this identifies a particular firm)
  *The American firm MCI, **which is the second largest US telecoms operator**, has formed an alliance with British Telecom.* (the relative clause is extra information and could be left out)
  *Mr Wells, **who is the CEO of the Harmer Group**, refused to speak to the press.* (the relative clause is extra information and could be left out)

PRACTICE

1 Finish the sentences about these famous people as in the example.
  Lazlo Biro was the man who made the first ball-point pen.

  1 Henry Ford/manufacture/mass-produced motor car
  2 Alexander Graham Bell/patent/telephone
  3 Nelson Mandela /become/black South African president
  4 John Logie Baird/produced/television pictures
  5 Elias Howe/invent/sewing machine

2 Make definitions from the sentence halves below.

1 A bear market is one in which	a unlisted securities are bought and sold
2 The black market is a market in which	b the supply of goods is plentiful
3 A buyer's market is one in which	c prices are tending to fall
4 The over-the-counter market is one in which	d raw materials are sold, often at a stated price for future delivery
5 A commodity market is one in which	e the sale of goods is not controlled by government order

3 Combine the sentences in an acceptable way, using a suitable relative pronoun. Be careful of the punctuation.

  1 He works for Quantum. Quantum is an American chemical company specialising in plastics.
  2 Sony has decided to produce a recordable digital video disc to replace the videocassette. Sony lost the videocassette war in the 1980s.
  3 The bank lent us the money. It went bust.
  4 The branch managers were all given a pay rise. They worked hard to get it.
  5 Imperial Tobacco is number two in the British cigarette market. Its operating profits are £350 million.
  6 They live in a city. The public transport network is excellent.
  7 We are making gains in productivity. They will make our company even more efficient.
  8 She offered to type up the report for me. It was kind of her.

17 Reported statements (1)

When reporting speech, we can either use 'direct' speech or 'indirect' speech.

1 We use direct speech when we quote the words that were used or reformulate them.

   Actual words: *My boss is not going to accept a 10% increase.'*

   Report: *So then he said, 'My boss is not going to accept a 10% increase.'*

2 In indirect speech, we make the speaker's words part of our sentence, changing pronouns and verb forms as necessary.

   He said (that) his boss was not going to accept a 10% increase.

Basic rules

1 What someone said at a particular time or place may be reported by another person in different circumstances. The tense used relates to the time when the report is made.

   Oh, hello, Jane, Bill has just phoned and he says he wants to speak to you about his trip to Rome.
   (the situation is present)

   James said that he didn't enjoy his interview. They insisted that he didn't have enough experience.
   (the interview took place some time ago)

2 After past reporting verbs, we normally put the tense of the verbs originally used one tense back in the past.

ORIGINAL VERBS	REPORTED VERBS
*'It **is** difficult for me to do.'*	*She **felt** it was difficult for her to do.*
*'She **is** getting the next flight.'*	*He said that she **was** getting the next flight.*
*'I**'ve** forgotten her name.'*	*He said he **had** forgotten her name.*
*'We **will** do our best.'*	*They said they **would** do their best.*
*'David **sent** you a fax.'*	*She said that David (**had**) **sent** me a fax.*

3 These modal verbs do not change.

*'You **could/might/ should** try to get in touch with them.'*	*She said that we **could/might/should** try to get in touch with them.*

PRACTICE

1 The second sentence is a reaction to what was said in the first. Match the two parts of each conversational exchange.

1 Would you like a game of chess?
2 Michael's waiting for us in the next room.
3 We will need to get everything translated.
4 I posted the cheque yesterday.
5 I'm visiting the production facility tomorrow.
6 I'll sell you it for half the price.

a I thought you said you were going next month.
b But you said you would give it to me for free.
c But I thought you could speak Spanish.
d But you said you didn't know how to play.
e But you said you had sent it ten days ago.
f I thought you said he had gone away.

2 These are some of the things that the CEO said at a meeting you attended a week ago. A colleague who was unable to attend wants you to tell him what she said.

1 Last year total sales amounted to $121m.

2 We will be investing more in R & D.

3 Our market share has grown by 18%.

4 I don't want to diversify in the immediate future.

5 Net profits this year should be in the region of $300m.

6 Nothing succeeds like success.

7 I am not planning to increase our debt-equity ratio.

18 Reported statements (2)

1 Note that *say* is more common with direct speech and *tell* is followed by the person who is told.
He **said**, '*Don't park there*'.
He **told** me not to park there.

2 *Tell* also means 'to instruct' or 'to inform'.
She **told** him to improve his performance.
She needs to **tell** you what time the meeting will be.

3 Changes of time and place and orientation can normally be indicated by changing the original words.

ORIGINAL WORDS	REPORTED WORDS
'I'll see you again **next week**.'	He said he'd see me **the following week** but he never came back.
'I'll ring you back **tomorrow**.'	He said he would ring me back **the following day**.
'I'm not going to sign **this** – it isn't what we agreed on at all.'	He said he wasn't going to sign **it/the contract** because it wasn't what they had agreed on.

4 Reporting verbs can be used to indicate the speaker's intention.

▌ *advise*, *warn* and *remind* are followed by a person object + infinitive.

'*If I were you, I'd leave early.*'
She **advised** <u>her colleague</u> **to leave** early.

'*Don't pay too high a price.*'
He **warned** <u>me</u> not **to pay** too high a price.

'*Don't forget to take your passport.*'
She **reminded** <u>him</u> **to take** his passport.

▌ *promise*, *threaten*, and *offer* are followed by an infinitive.

'*I'll be in touch soon.*'
He **promised** <u>to be</u> in touch soon.

'*We'll sue you if you use our brand name.*'
They **threatened** <u>to sue</u> us if we used their brand name.

'*I'll give you a hand if you like.*'
She **offered** <u>to give</u> me a hand.

▌ *suggest* and *recommend* are followed by the *-ing* form.

'*Why don't you try a different supplier?*'
She **suggested** <u>trying</u> a different supplier.

PRACTICE

1 Complete the sentences, using *say, tell, said*, and *told*.

1 Anita has just phoned to _____ she can't come to the conference.

2 Did she _____ you how she was going to raise extra capital?

3 It was John Kennedy who _____ : 'Ask not what your country can do for you; ask what you can do for your country.'

4 He _____ the committee that the chairman had never been involved in corruption.

5 The CEO has _____ the Financial Controller to make economies.

2 Using a dictionary if necessary, divide these verbs into two groups: ones followed by *that* and ones followed by *to*.
feel   offer   insist   point out   promise   say   tell   threaten

VERBS FOLLOWED BY *THAT*	VERBS FOLLOWED BY *TO*

3 Transform the direct speech into reported speech using the verbs in italics.

1 'I'm not accepting 10%. No way!'
He refused …

2 'I think you should seek legal advice.'
She recommended …

3 'Don't buy shares in BIY, they're about to go into liquidation.'
He warned …

4 'Would you like me to get you a taxi?'
She offered …

5 'I'll send you a copy of the feasibility study.'
He promised …

6 'We'll withdraw from the project if you deal with our competitors.'
They threatened …

7 'OK, I'll increase your budget allocation.'
She agreed …

8 'Initial profit projections appear to be favourable.'
He claimed …

19 Reported questions

1 When we report yes/no questions, we use *if* or *whether* and make any necessary tense changes.
'**Will** you be going to the summer party?'
She asked me **if** I **would** be going to the summer party.

'**Can** I see him at five o'clock?'
He wanted to know **if** he **could** see you at five o'clock.

'**Were** you by any chance born in India?'
He wondered **whether** I **was** born in India.

2 When the original question begins with a question word (i.e. *which, what, where, why, when, how*, etc.), we report these questions using a different word order: verb + subject changes to subject + verb.

ORIGINAL QUESTION	REPORTED QUESTION
'Which airport are you leaving from?'	He asked me which airport I was leaving from.
'How old are you?'	He wanted to know how old I am/was.

3 The auxiliaries *do, does* and *did* are not used in the reported question

'Where **do** you live?'	He asked me where I lived.
(**NOT** He asked me where ~~do I live.~~)	
'How much **did** it cost?'	He wanted to know how much it cost.
(**NOT** He wanted to know how much ~~did it cost.~~)	
'What time **will** the shuttle leave.'	He asked her what time the shuttle would leave.
(**NOT** He asked her what time ~~would the shuttle leave.~~)	
'Who **did** you talk to?'	He wanted to know who I'd talked to.
(**NOT** He wanted to know ~~who did I talk to.~~)	

There is no question mark in the reported question.

4 The same word order principle applies in questions beginning with *Do you know* or *Could you tell me.*
Do you know where the station is?

PRACTICE

1 These are some of the questions that were asked during a job interview for a post in an American firm.

Report these questions using 'They wanted to know ...' and 'They asked me if/whether ...'

1 Where did you see the advertisement?
2 Why are you interested in joining our firm?
3 What attracted you to the post?
4 How long ago did you leave ICI?
5 How well did you get on with your colleagues?
6 Do you know how to use EXCEL?
7 Can you speak English?
8 What other languages can you speak?
9 Do you have the TOEFL or TOEIC?
10 Do you have any friends living in the USA?
11 How soon can you start?

2 You have been taking messages for a colleague who has been on a trip abroad for the last two weeks. He is now in your office and you are briefing him on what has been happening in his absence.

1 While you were out...
Mr Vaughan:
'How many items do we have to sell before we reach break-even point?'

2 While you were out...
Mr Pozetti:
'How soon will the laboratory samples be ready?'

3 While you were out...
Mrs Cole:
'When did we last review the complaints procedure?'

4 While you were out...
Christine:
'Should we take out political risk insurance for the Albanian consignment?'

5 While you were out...
Herr Lüdcke:
'How long does the guarantee last?'

6 While you were out...
Richard:
'Which car hire firm do we normally use?'

7 While you were out...
Elaine:
'Who is responsible for authorising expenses?'

8 While you were out...
Dorothy:
'When was the last time we had an order from Patagonia?'

9 While you were out...
Mr Gould:
'Could you please check the specifications for order no. 549/Y?'

20 Verb + -ing or to-infinitive

It is common for a verb to be followed by another verb. But it is often difficult to know whether the second verb is a *to*-infinitive or terminated by *-ing*.

1 These verbs are followed by a *verb + -ing* but not a *to*-infinitive.

admit	avoid	consider	count on	delay	enjoy
finish	imagine	involve	justify	look forward to
miss	mind	postpone	recommend	risk

Have you **considered** work**ing** from home?
The new design will **involve** chang**ing** the packaging.
The situation doesn't **justify** tak**ing** legal action.
We **postponed** launch**ing** the new model.
We **look forward to** see**ing** you soon.
We **risk** los**ing** our position as market leader.

2 The following verbs take a *to*-infinitive.

afford	appear	arrange	attempt	claim
decide	demand	expect	fail	guarantee
hesitate	hope	manage	offer	plan
proceed	promise	tend	undertake	wish

Please **arrange to transfer** the money to our account.
I **expect to see** you in Shanghai shortly.
We **plan to open** a new branch in Brazil.
We **promise to replace** any damaged items.
They **refused to give** us credit.
We do not **wish to be** involved in the deal.

3 Some verbs are followed by either an infinitive or another verb + *-ing*. Sometimes there is a change in meaning as in the examples below.

We do not **allow/authorise** smoking on our premises.
(= in general)
She **allowed/authorised** him to smoke a cigar in the office. (= on this specific occasion)

I will never **forget** meeting Bill Gates.
(= I will always remember)
I often **forget** to turn off my mobile phone.
(= fail to remember)

I **mean** to see her later this week.
(= I intend to)
I could get a better job but it would **mean** moving.
(= involve)

They **stopped** sending us junk mail after a while.
(= they ceased)
She **stopped** to have a cigarette.
(to = so as to)

PRACTICE

1 Put the verb in brackets into the correct form.

1 The staff were asked to avoid (speak) to journalists.
2 The firm attempted (take over) its nearest competitor.
3 We cannot count on (remain) market leader forever.
4 We had to delay (launch) the new product.
5 I have arranged (be) replaced during my absence.
6 She doesn't mind (work) overtime if it's paid.
7 I hope (see) you again in the near future.
8 He actually enjoys (travel) over 20 hours a week.
9 We guarantee (provide) total quality.
10 Personally, I can't afford (buy) a Rolls Royce.
11 Would you mind (wait) a few minutes?
12 I never wished (appear) rude.
13 We promise (refund) your money if you are not entirely satisfied.
14 Since I left England, I miss (go out) for a pub lunch.
15 She tends (believe) that governments should not interfere in the free market.
16 The bank has undertaken (back) us in the venture.
17 Have you ever considered (move) abroad?
18 We don't expect conditions (improve) for some time.
19 She offered (give) me a lift to the airport.
20 At first Elias Howe failed (get) people interested in his new sewing machine.

2 Complete the following letter.

Dear Mr Magnusson,

Further to your phone call, I confirm that we cannot afford (purchase)[1] the furniture at the price you propose. However, if you could arrange (reduce)[2] your price by 5%, we would undertake (make)[3] an initial order of 50 office desks and swivel chairs. If you agree, we would not mind (pay)[4] at 30 rather than 60 days.

I hope (hear)[5] from you soon and look forward (receive)[6] your acceptance of this proposal.

Yours,

Powerhouse transcript

1 connections

GRAMMAR REVIEW   page 6
Two business failures

THE OFFICE

RADCLIFFE	Morning, Jill.
JILL	Morning, Mr Radcliffe. Oh, I'm afraid you can't go in there.
RADCLIFFE	What do you mean?
JILL	Well, they're having a meeting.
RADCLIFFE	I know they're having a meeting. We have a meeting in there every Monday at this time.
JILL	Yes, but this week ... it's a bit different.
RADCLIFFE	Don't be ridiculous. Out of my way. I'm going in.
JILL	No, Mr Radcliffe, I'm sorry. You see ... they're ... well, they're having the meeting without you this week, Mr Radcliffe.
RADCLIFFE	But, Jill, I always go to these meetings.
THOMAS	Are you having a few problems, Jill?
JILL	It's ... um ...
THOMAS	Ah, Bill ...
RADCLIFFE	What's going on? I always come to these meetings.
THOMAS	Yes, Bill, I know. But, well, you've been here a long time ...
RADCLIFFE	What? I ... What are you saying?

THE MOBILE PHONE

JOHN   Hello? Oh, hello, Clara. Oh, just a second, the traffic's moving ... Sorry about that. Yes. Well, I'm afraid I'm having a few problems this morning ... Yes. I'm sitting in the car on the ring road. And, well, it's not moving ... not much, anyway ... No, this doesn't happen every time ... Oh, you know me better than that. I come to you every month at the same time ... Yes. Yes, I know lots of other people are selling the same things as me ... Yes, and I know you always give me a big order ... Listen, I'm sitting in a traffic jam, what can I do? ... Well, buy from the other person then ... No, no, I'm only joking. I don't mean that. Clara? Clara, are you still there?

DOING BUSINESS 2   page 10
Not getting through!

CONVERSATION 1

GEORGE	Hello. Could I speak to Dr Lowenstein, please?
WOMAN 1	Just a moment, please. ... Hello. I'm afraid that Dr Lowenstein's on another line at the moment.
GEORGE	Can I hold?
WOMAN 1	Sure. ... Dr Lowenstein's line is still busy. Do you still want to hold?
GEORGE	No, thanks. I'll call back later.

CONVERSATION 2

GEORGE	Could you put me through to Dr Lowenstein, please?
WOMAN 2	No, I'm sorry, Mr Lowenstein is not available right now. Mr Lowenstein groups his calls and will receive calls any time after three.
GEORGE	I'm sorry, could you speak more slowly?
WOMAN 2	Oh. Yes. I'm sorry. I said Mr Lowenstein is not available. Could you call back after three?
GEORGE	Can I leave a message?
WOMAN 2	No problem.

CONVERSATION 3

GEORGE	Could I speak to Dr Lowenstein, please?
MAN 1	I'm sorry, can you speak up?
GEORGE	Can I speak to Dr Lowenstein, please?
MAN 1	Sorry, caller, it's a bad line. Can you call back?
GEORGE	OK. Bye.

CONVERSATION 4

GEORGE	Dr Lowenstein, please.
MAN 2	Lowenstein?
GEORGE	Yes. Could you put me through to him?
MAN 2	Ah. I think you've got the wrong number.
GEORGE	Oh. I am sorry.

CONVERSATION 5

GEORGE	Can I speak to Dr Lowenstein, please?
MAN 3	Oh, I'm sorry, Dr Lowenstein has left the company.
GEORGE	Ah.
MAN 3	Would you like to speak to the new man, Mr Smythe?
GEORGE	Sorry? Can you spell that for me?
MAN 3	Yes. Smythe. S.M.Y.T.H.E. Shall I put you through?
GEORGE	Yes, please.

MAN 3   Can I ask who's calling, please?
GEORGE   Yes. It's George Coy from Newhaven ...

SOCIAL SKILLS page 14
Alternative versions

CONVERSATION 1

BUXTON   Hmmm ... It's been a long day. What are you drinking?
ROBERTS   Gimlet.
BUXTON   Well, let's have a couple more. I'm sorry, we haven't been introduced.
ROBERTS   Roberts. Ian Roberts.
BUXTON   I'm Michael Buxton. How do you do.
ROBERTS   How do you do.

CONVERSATION 2

BUXTON   Hmmm ... It's been a long day. What are you drinking?
ROBERTS   Gimlet.
BUXTON   Well, let's have a couple more. May I introduce myself? I'm Michael Buxton. And you must be Ian Roberts.
ROBERTS   That's right. I'm pleased to meet you.

2 the **company**

GRAMMAR REVIEW page 18
A job description

JULIAN   That's right. I'm the general manager of the institute, which means ... well, basically, it means I do everything. I mean I don't have to repair the equipment, but apart from that I ... well, I have to prepare the budgets, recruit new staff, conduct performance appraisals and so on. And obviously, as this is a nuclear research institute, health and safety is, like, big big news – so I have to check all the health and safety procedures on a very regular basis. But, of course, I'm not a scientist, so I don't actually have to find new uses for radioactive material or anything like that. And, obviously, I'm office-based, so I don't have to go out to foreign markets and sell our ideas or ... I don't know ... er ... is that what you want to know?

GRAMMAR REVIEW page 19
Safety procedures

JULIAN   Right, this is the rest area. Oh, excuse me, we have to keep this door closed at all times, I'm afraid. Now, obviously you don't have to wear protective clothing or anything like that in here, and you don't have to wear the special shoes, either. But I'm afraid you mustn't bring any food or drink into this area ... oh, and of course, you mustn't smoke. If you've got any questions, you will ask, won't you?

DOING BUSINESS 1 page 21
Formal and informal meetings

HARRIET   Right. Are we all here? Good, well, let's get down to business. I think our objective is pretty clear. We're here today to sort out this ... this mess. We have to decide what we're going to do about the problems with our travel bookings. I don't know ... it's, well ... it's chaos.
PATTI   Sorry, Harriet. What do you mean by that?
HARRIET   What do I mean? Patti, I mean it looks like we're going to have to cancel our regional sales conference and, on top of that, we're going to lose $25,000 or more.
PATTI   It's not chaos, Harriet, it's a problem. OK?
HARRIET   OK, it's a problem. And we're here today to solve it. Now I've got another meeting at three, so I'm going to have to set a time limit of, say, 2.45. Is that OK with everybody?
    ...
BRIAN   Can I say something here?
HARRIET   Sure.
BRIAN   Is someone taking minutes?
HARRIET   Minutes. Yes. Thanks, Brian ... Mike, can you take the minutes?
MIKE   I am already.
HARRIET   Brilliant. Thank you. Right. Before we start, are there any questions? Mike?
MIKE   Yes, I'm sorry, Harriet, can you repeat what you said about the money?
HARRIET   I said ... I said we're going to lose $25,000, which is true ...

DOING BUSINESS 2 page 22
A discussion

HARRIET   Right, let's move on to the next point, shall we? Violence in the workplace, I'm afraid. Again.
BRIAN   Disgrace.
HARRIET   It's the third assault on a member of our staff this year. I don't know what we're going to do. Has anyone got any ideas?
PATTI   Well, for a start, why don't you have a clear company policy on violence? That way, at least our people will know where they stand – if they're ever threatened.
HARRIET   Thanks, Patti. Yes. Good point. I ... um ...
MIKE   Can I say something here?
HARRIET   Yes, Mike. What do you think?
MIKE   Have you thought about these training courses?
BRIAN   Training courses.
MIKE   Yes. They're courses where you learn to see the danger signs, to ... well, to try to stay in control of the situation.
HARRIET   Hmm. I'll look into it.
BRIAN   I ... er ...
HARRIET   Yes. Sorry, Brian, what's your view?
BRIAN   Well, it's quite simple. I think you should just tell people to use their common sense.
HARRIET   Well, thanks ...

DOING BUSINESS 2   **page 22**
Making your point

PATTI   Well, for a start, I think you should have a clear company policy on violence. That way, at least our people will know where they stand – if they're ever threatened.

MIKE   Why don't you send people on training courses?

BRIAN   It's quite simple. Have you thought about just telling people to use their common sense?

3 money

GRAMMAR REVIEW   **page 31**
The Paul Reichmann story

The Canadian property developer, Paul Reichmann, was once described as the Einstein of the business world. At its peak, his company, Olympia & York, had $25 billion in assets, including 40 huge office blocks around the world. But, in 1992, a time when property markets were experiencing a serious slump, the company collapsed. Reichmann and his family lost perhaps as much as $10 billion in just five years.

Reichmann's career is the story of a business genius, ready to take bigger and bigger risks. But, in his early years, a career in business seemed most unlikely. In fact, Olympia & York was started by his brothers, while Paul was working on religious and educational projects in north Africa – and he didn't join the company until he was 26 years old. But, when he did, his talent as a property developer was soon obvious to everyone.

After two hugely successful projects in Toronto, he started doing business in New York in 1977 and, in 1980, made perhaps his greatest business decision. That was when Olympia & York bought a site in the south of Manhattan Island and started work on one of New York's biggest developments – the World Financial Center. The project made the Reichmanns the largest property owners in the city. Builders were still finishing work on the World Financial Center, when Paul Reichmann made his next huge deal. On the other side of the Atlantic, Margaret Thatcher's government was trying to develop a large area of derelict land to the east of London. In 1987, Reichmann bought the site and work began on the 24 buildings known as Canary Wharf. But the timing was all wrong. In 1989, there was a dramatic slump in the London property market. By 1991, Olympia & York's debts were $20 billion and, in 92, the company collapsed.

But that was not the end of Paul Reichmann. In 1995, he was part of another group of investors which bought back Canary Wharf and turned it into a remarkable success – which shows that, although Paul Reichmann may not be a business Einstein, he's certainly a man who doesn't give up.

DOING BUSINESS 1   **page 32**
Stress

1

O o	o O	O o	o O
Thirty.	Thirteen.	Forty.	Fourteen.

2

A   Forty. Thirteen. Thirty. Fifty.
B   Sorry. Was that fifteen?
A   No, fifty.
B   Right.
A   Seventy. Seventeen. Eighteen.
B   Eighty?
A   No, eighteen.
B   Thank you.
A   And, finally, nineteen, eighteen, ninety.
B   Nineteen, eighteen, ninety. Great.

DOING BUSINESS 2   **page 34**
Black Monday

The breakfast news on Tuesday, 18 October 1987.
Yesterday was the worst day on the stock market this century. In London, share values fell by around £50 billion; on Wall Street, the Dow Jones index plunged 508 points – a drop of over 20%.

Share values had soared to new highs this autumn and for weeks analysts had been predicting that the bull market couldn't last. But when the crash came the market fell more dramatically than anyone had imagined.

Today, everyone is hoping that the situation will stabilise and that markets will recover quickly. In the last major stock market crash in 1929, the market fell by just 10% and that led to the great depression – a time when hundreds of banks failed, thousands of businesses closed and millions of people lost their jobs.

DOING BUSINESS 2   **page 35**
Sound and spelling

closed, increased, lasted, collapsed, crashed, decided, intended, invested, peaked, plunged, predicted, recovered, slumped, soared, stabilised

SOCIAL SKILLS   **page 38**
Do you come here often?

FRANK   So, where are you from?
ANNA   Dallas. I'm American.
FRANK   Oh. And how long are you here for?
ANNA   Just a couple of weeks.
FRANK   Hmmm. What are you doing here?
ANNA   I'm thinking of getting into computer programming. So I'm visiting quite a few companies like yours.

FRANK   Really? And what are you going to do in your spare time?

ANNA   Well, I love art galleries, so I'll try to visit quite a few while I'm here ... Do you like art?

FRANK   Not quite my thing, I'm afraid ... Oh, by the way, I didn't catch your name.

ANNA   Anna. Anna Keefe.

4 the **market**

Marketing VOCABULARY   page 41
Sound and spelling

Marlborough, tough, rough, Edinburgh, through, cough, although

GRAMMAR REVIEW   page 42
A launch checklist

CHRIS   Ah, Kate. Is everything ready for the launch next month?

KATE   Well, we're doing OK, I think.

CHRIS   Have you booked the hotel?

KATE   Yes, I have. I booked it ... ooh, last Thursday.

CHRIS   And have you sent out invitations?

KATE   No, not yet, I'm afraid.

CHRIS   Hmm. Have you made the travel arrangements?

KATE   Yes. I did that last week.

CHRIS   Good. What about the audio-visual equipment? Have you organised that yet?

KATE   Ah, no, I haven't. Thank you for reminding me.

CHRIS   Oh, and one more thing. Have you spoken to Joan about the catering?

KATE   Yes, I have. I spoke to her yesterday, in fact.

CHRIS   Good. Well, it sounds like it's coming on, anyway. Keep me posted, though, won't you ...

DOING BUSINESS 1   page 44
A photocopier salesman

JONES   Now, Mr Allen, come in and take a seat.

ALLEN   No, thanks, Mr Jones, I prefer to stand. You see, I haven't come here to waste your time, so I'll come straight to the point. Now, I can see you're looking at my pen here, aren't you? Normally retails at £45, that does. But I'll tell you what, because I like your face, it's yours – for nothing. That's right, F.R.E.E. free. And that's not all I'm going to do, Mr Jones. As well as this free pen, I'm going to offer you the unique opportunity to own our new top-of-the-range colour photocopier. Just take thirty seconds of your valuable time to look through our newly published brochure and I guarantee you'll be convinced ...

DOING BUSINESS 2   page 47
Four acceptances

ACCEPTANCE 1

That seems like a reasonable offer, which I accept on behalf of my family. I look forward to doing business with you. And I want to thank you for considering my family in your business plans.

ACCEPTANCE 2

I can see that you are a serious man and I think we have the basis of an understanding. But, clearly, there are many details for us to discuss. Now ...

ACCEPTANCE 3

OK, it's a deal. Now I hope you'll join with me in a small ... er ... celebration of our new relationship.

ACCEPTANCE 4

Yeah. I like the sound of the idea, but I think you can do better ... out of respect for me and for my family, you understand. Now tell me a little bit more about what you can do for us ...

SOCIAL SKILLS   page 51
Making an arrangement

WOMAN   Hello.

MAN   Hi, remember me?

WOMAN   Oh, yes, of course I do. Hello.

MAN   Listen, it's about the shoot. Can we fix a time? My daughter's coming to stay.

WOMAN   Oh, I'm sorry, I can't tell you at the moment. We'll have to get the copy agreed, the director lined up and so on. How about a month from now at the earliest?

MAN   Try and bring a schedule when you come round with the copy.

WOMAN   Right. I'll get the men in suits working on it. It'll be great to meet you.

MAN   It'll be great to meet you, too.

WOMAN   Would you like to have lunch? It's on me.

5 **management**

GRAMMAR REVIEW   page 54
A staff meeting

WORKER 1   I think the thing we all want to know about is job security. Are there going to be redundancies?

MANAGER   No, now let me make this clear. Nobody is going to lose their job under the reorganisation.

WORKER 2   When are we going to get a decision on the new bonus scheme?

MANAGER   Yes. Well, you'll probably hear something from us next week.

WORKER 3   And what about the new health and safety arrangements?

MANAGER   Good question. We'll decide that at the management meeting at the end of the month.

WORKER 1   Are we going to get shorter working hours?

MANAGER   No, I'm afraid you're certainly not going to get that. Now, are there any more questions? Yes, Philippa ...?

DOING BUSINESS 1   page 57
Meet the staff

LEORA   So, Ben, tell me, do you like the new arrangements in the office?

BEN   No opinion, really. I liked my old desk; the new one's OK. My old computer didn't work properly; my new one doesn't either.

LEORA   Ah. I see. Right. And how do you feel about the new management structure?

BEN   Makes no difference to me, I just do my job.

LEORA   Well, good, I suppose that's good, anyway. So is staff morale reasonably high, then?

BEN   Oh, yeah. Sure.

LEORA   Anything you'd like to add?

BEN   No, no, it's good, morale's OK.

LEORA   Hmm. Have you got any special training needs?

BEN   No. I know my job. No problem there.

LEORA   So are you happy with the department's progress over the past year?

BEN   Happy? Progress? Huh. Now this is going to take some time, so I hope you're ready. Are you ready?

LEORA   Well, I suppose so, yes ...

BEN   In my view, and this goes for a lot of us out there, we've had enough of management interfering with something that's worked perfectly well for years ...

DOING BUSINESS 2   page 59
Interviewing the major

INTERVIEWER   So, Major, can we start by talking about the skills that you can bring to this job?

MAJOR   That's no problem.

INTERVIEWER   Now, obviously, as an army major you've got plenty of managerial experience, but how do you try to motivate the people that you manage?

MAJOR   Hmm. Well, a little bit of carrot and plenty of stick. That's my way.

INTERVIEWER   A little bit of carrot and plenty of stick?

MAJOR   Yes. What I mean is, you have to be tough with the people you manage, make them respect you. And sometimes ... once in a while, you can give them a little incentive.

INTERVIEWER   I see. Would you say that you're a natural communicator?

MAJOR   A natural communicator? No. Not really.

INTERVIEWER   Can you give me an example of a situation in which your communication skills were particularly important?

MAJOR   Hmm. That's tricky.

INTERVIEWER   Well, tell me about how you deal with a difficult soldier.

MAJOR   Oh, that's easy. Shout at him, punish him and make sure he knows his place.

INTERVIEWER   Right. Yes. Well, er ... let's talk a little about your experience. What did you like most about your time in the army?

MAJOR   Oh, the discipline.

INTERVIEWER   The discipline?

MAJOR   Yes, the combination of the discipline and the adventure. I love it.

INTERVIEWER   So why are you leaving?

MAJOR   Well, I suppose I'm looking for a new challenge ... and more money, of course.

INTERVIEWER   Challenges are obviously important to you. Tell me something more about yourself. How do you spend your free time?

MAJOR   I like to keep fit. Very, very fit. I like to be outside, running, hunting, having a good time.

INTERVIEWER   Well, there are plenty of those kind of opportunities in Kenya.

MAJOR   I know. That's why I want the job ... one of the reasons, of course.

INTERVIEWER   And what do you think are your weak points?

MAJOR   Weak? That's not my kind of adjective. I'm ... er ... I'm ... I know ... I'm not very good with young children.

INTERVIEWER   I see. So, major, let's talk about what you want from the company. How much do you expect to earn?

MAJOR   No less than US$80,000 per year.

INTERVIEWER   Right. And finally, what about the future? What kind of job would you like to have in five years' time?

MAJOR   Five years' time? I'd like to retire! Ha ha ha! Only kidding! No, I never think that far ahead.

INTERVIEWER   Well, thank you, major. Now do you have any questions ...

SOCIAL SKILLS   page 62
Oh, really?

1   MAN Have you heard that the price of phone calls is going to fall dramatically?

WOMAN   Really?

2   MAN Someone told me that we're all going to do our shopping by computer within a few years.

WOMAN   Really?

3   MAN Apparently, an American company is taking bookings for holidays in space.

WOMAN   Really?

4 MAN Did you know that scientists are developing ways of building skyscrapers out of diamonds?
WOMAN Really?

5 MAN I heard that Ferrari are bringing out a new sports car next year.
WOMAN Really?

SOCIAL SKILLS page 63
That's interesting

1 MAN Have you heard that the price of phone calls is going to fall dramatically?
WOMAN That's interesting.

2 MAN Someone told me that we're all going to do our shopping by computer within a few years.
WOMAN That sounds great.

3 MAN Apparently, an American company is taking bookings for holidays in space.
WOMAN How strange.

4 MAN Did you know that scientists are developing ways of building skyscrapers out of diamonds?
WOMAN I don't believe you.

5 MAN I heard that Ferrari are bringing out a new sports car next year.
WOMAN Is that right?

SOCIAL SKILLS page 63
Finding out more

MAN Did you know that scientists are developing ways of building skyscrapers out of diamonds?
WOMAN I don't believe you.
MAN It's true.
WOMAN What do you mean?
MAN Well, it's nanotechnology.
WOMAN Nanotechnology?
MAN The science of very small things. Scientists are learning how to manipulate individual atoms to create completely new kinds of material.
WOMAN Oh. Is that right?
MAN Yes. So, in theory, you see, there's nothing to stop people building skyscrapers out of diamonds ...
WOMAN Sorry to change the subject, but have you seen my newspaper?

6 the **customer**

GRAMMAR REVIEW page 66
A loan adviser

CUSTOMER So, if I borrow £3,000, how much will I have to pay back in total?
SALESWOMAN Well, if you borrow £3,000 over three years, it'll be £3,831. If you want to borrow for longer, it'll be slightly more.
CUSTOMER So, how much are the monthly repayments?
SALESWOMAN Well, if you take a three-year option, that'll be ... £106 per month.
CUSTOMER Hmm. That sounds good.
SALESWOMAN There is something else I'd like to mention.
CUSTOMER Yes?
SALESWOMAN Well, I know that it's not a very pleasant thought, but, well ... what would happen if you lost your job? Would you still be able to meet the repayments?
CUSTOMER Hmm. I ... er ...
SALESWOMAN And what about if you were seriously ill ... or even if you died, would your family be able to pay back this loan?
CUSTOMER I don't see what you're saying.
SALESWOMAN Well, we normally advise our borrowers to take out some kind of insurance on their loan. So if anything happens to you, you won't have to worry about your loan repayments.
CUSTOMER Listen, if anything bad happened to me, the last thing I'd worry about would be my loan repayments.
SALESWOMAN So you're saying you don't want to participate in our loan protection scheme.
CUSTOMER That's right. I think I can live with just a little bit of risk.

GRAMMAR REVIEW page 67
Elision

1 WOMAN What will you do if it rains this weekend?
MAN Ooh, if it rains, I'll probably stay at home.

2 MAN What would you do if another company offered you a job with a much bigger salary?
WOMAN Well, if I was offered more money, I certainly wouldn't say no!

3 WOMAN What will you do if your boss asks you to work late tomorrow?
MAN Tomorrow? Tomorrow evening? I won't do it. I can't. I'm going out.

4 WOMAN   What would you do if you found a burglar in your house after work this evening?

  MAN   I don't know ... I'd scream ... No, I wouldn't. I'd call the police ... from the phone box round the corner, of course.

5 MAN   What would happen to your company if the price of oil doubled?

  WOMAN   If it doubled? Oh, we'd probably go bankrupt, wouldn't we?

DOING BUSINESS 1 page 69
A photocopier salesman

BELEW   Well, Mr Jones, I'll tell you what. We've got a special offer on at the moment. Now, what this means is, if you buy this copier from me today, I'll give you a two-year guarantee and 15% off the normal purchase price. How does that sound to you?

JONES   Hmmm. Well, it's tempting, but if I bought a new photocopier now, my bank manager would go crazy.

BELEW   What would you say if I offered you six months interest-free credit?

JONES   Six months? Interest-free? OK. If you give me a two-year guarantee, 15% off and six months' interest-free credit, I'll take one.

BELEW   Right, well, let's sort out the paperwork ...

SOCIAL SKILLS page 75
A few questions about the menu

WAITER   Are you ready to order?

  MAN   Well, actually, we've got a few questions about the menu.

WAITER   Of course.

WOMAN   What do you mean by 'Mixed things'?

WAITER   Yes. That's not very clear, is it? It's ... erm ... well, it's a kind of salad, but with little pieces of ... sort of bread, do you know what I mean?

  MAN   Yes. I think you mean Waldorf salad. That's what we call it, anyway. Waldorf salad.

WAITER   Hmm. Waldorf salad.

WOMAN   And how exactly is the trout cooked?

WAITER   Well, we put it under the grill with ... erm ... little nuts.

WOMAN   Grilled trout with almonds.

WAITER   If you say so ...

  MAN   And what's a 'grilled leg of salmon'? Is that some kind of joke?

WAITER   A joke? ... Oh, I see ... Well ... actually, yes. Yes, it is.

  MAN   Presumably you mean grilled salmon steak or something like that, do you?

WAITER   Yes, I suppose we do. Although there is another problem with that.

  MAN   What's that, then?

WAITER   The salmon's off.

  MAN   Oh ... I ... er ... Well. So, what shall we have?

WOMAN   Umm ... well, it's tricky, isn't it? What do you recommend?

WAITER   Well, the slice of pig is wonderful.

  MAN   Slice of pig? What are you talking about?

7 production

GRAMMAR REVIEW page 78
The Hawthorne Experiments

The Hawthorne experiments? Yes. Extremely interesting. They were conducted by Elton Mayo in the ... the 1920s, I believe. It was at Western Electric's Hawthorne Works in Chicago ... hence the name. More than 20,000 workers were involved.

   In the first experiment, the lighting conditions in the Hawthorne factory were improved – and it was found that output also improved. In the second experiment, the lighting conditions were made worse. Surprisingly, output went up again. Finally, lighting conditions in the factory were returned to normal. And do you know what? Once again, the workers' productivity improved. Quite extraordinary, really. So what did Elton Mayo make of all this? Hmm. Well, what conclusion would you draw?

GRAMMAR REVIEW page 78
The Hawthorne Effect

Yes, well, Elton Mayo's conclusion was quite interesting really. He believed that the increases in productivity had nothing to do with the changes in lighting conditions at all. Output had increased because the workers felt valued and they felt valued simply because they were part of an experiment.

GRAMMAR REVIEW page 79
Comparing processes

Okay. Well, our burgers are made like this. First, the meat is taken out of the freezer ... that's obvious, really ... and it's cooked under the grill. Now, our buns aren't heated, so as soon as the meat's ready, it's put straight into the cold bun. Oh, I should say, that normally a batch of six burgers is made at a time. Right. Now next the burgers are dressed – with lettuce, tomato, cheese and so on. Finally, the burgers are put it into special little boxes so the heat is kept in and then they're slid down a chute into the serving bin near the counter. And I guess that's about it.

SOCIAL SKILLS page 87
Talking about interests

EXTRACT 1

  MAN   So, what do you do in your spare time?

WOMAN   Well, I'm pretty busy, as you can imagine, but, when I get a chance, I try and go to the cinema.

MAN	Really? Have you seen the new Spielberg movie yet?
WOMAN	No, I haven't actually.
MAN	Oh, you should go. I think it's great.
WOMAN	What did you like about it?
MAN	Well, you remember Schindler's List? It's got the same kind of feel ...

EXTRACT 2

WOMAN	Are you interested in sport?
MAN	Yeah, I love it, but I'm getting a bit old for it now.
WOMAN	What do you play?
MAN	Football. Five-a-side football, twice a week after work.
WOMAN	How do you find that?
MAN	Exhausting. That's why I say I'm getting too old.

EXTRACT 3

MAN	Did you watch the news this morning?
WOMAN	Yes, I did.
MAN	Did you see the report on customer service in the business news?
WOMAN	Yes, I did. I didn't like it much, though. What do you think?
MAN	Well, it's funny, I know the guy who made that ...

8 business and society

DOING BUSINESS 2   page 94
Comparing presentations

PRESENTATION 1

Right. Good. Well, perhaps I'll start, shall I? Can you hear me all right? Good. Now ... erm ... probably the most important thing I've got to say is that ... well, the company's results are looking pretty good this year. Have you all seen the graph of sales figures? No? Well, I've got one here. There you are. Can you see this all right at the back? No? Well, you'll have to take my word for it, then. Results are good. Yes. Very good, actually. But, anyway, I'll tell you a bit more about that in a minute. Now, where was I? Um ... let's start with what's happening at the moment. Would that be a good idea?

PRESENTATION 2

Good morning, ladies and gentlemen. I'm here today to tell you about our company's financial position. I've divided my presentation into four parts. Firstly, I want to talk about the current financial situation. Secondly, I'd like to examine our performance over the past year. Thirdly, I'll look at our prospects for the next twelve months. Finally, I'll make some recommendations. I'll be happy to answer questions at the end of my presentation.

Right. I'd like you to look at this graph ...

9 business ethics

GRAMMAR REVIEW   page 103
Pronunciation

If I had heard about the offer, I would have bought the vacuum cleaner.
If I'*d* heard about the offer, I would've bought the vacuum cleaner.
If I'*d* heard about the offer, I'd have bought the vacuum cleaner.

GRAMMAR REVIEW   page 103
Hoover's reaction

WOMAN	Well, of course, Hoover could have said that the special offer was a joke – but I don't think that would have worked.
MAN	They could have delayed a decision for as long as possible – until people had forgotten about it – it's possible, I suppose. Or they could have offered people a cheaper gift – I don't know what exactly, but they could have done something like that.
WOMAN	Or, of course, they could have given all the applicants the free flights that they were promised.
MAN	And that's what they should have done ... from the ethical point of view.
WOMAN	Yeah, you're right, I suppose, although I'm not sure that's what I would have done.
MAN	Well, what would you have done?
WOMAN	Oh, I'd probably have waited until people had forgotten about it ...
MAN	Would you?
WOMAN	Well, yes ...

DOING BUSINESS 1   page 104
Signposting

EXTRACT 1

This is a graph of the company's turnover during the past three months. As you can see, sales rose slightly in April and May before falling sharply in June.

EXTRACT 2

The company's sales of traditional English sausages have fallen by over 37% in its three largest supermarkets in the north of England during the past six months.

EXTRACT 3

The company must change its product range and improve its image if it wants to survive – which is why the right advertising targeted at the right customer is so important.

EXTRACT 4

Frankly, the company's attitude reminds me of something a journalist once said to me, 'You can never underestimate the intelligence of the general public.' Well, in this case, I think that's just what the company has done. But let me get back to my main point.

DOING BUSINESS 1   **page 105**
A list of three

EXTRACT 1

All right, ladies, I'm not asking for £100, I'm not asking for £75. Ladies, this beautiful dress is yours for just £50. So, who'll be my first customer?

EXTRACT 2

Our customers aren't just asking for the cheapest prices. They're not just asking for the best quality. They are asking for the cheapest prices *and* the best quality and, believe me, they will accept nothing less. So, how can we make sure that we give them what they want?

DOING BUSINESS 2   **page 107**
Emphasis

The *point* is, ladies and gentlemen, that *greed*, for lack of a better word, is *good*.

SOCIAL SKILLS   **page 110**
Sounding polite

CONVERSATION 1
MAN	Can I invite you to dinner this evening?
WOMAN	Thank you. That's very kind of you.

CONVERSATION 2
MAN	Thanks very much for everything. I'd like you to have this.
WOMAN	I'm sorry, but my company doesn't allow me to accept gifts.

CONVERSATION 3
WOMAN	Would you like to go to the concert tonight?
MAN	That's very kind of you, but I must refuse.

10 the **digital revolution**

Hi-tech VOCABULARY   **page 113**
Word stress

1	WOMAN	the software industry
	MAN	the software industry

2	WOMAN	television, television
	MAN	video-conferencing, video-conferencing
	WOMAN	optical fibre, optical fibre
	MAN	cable TV, cable TV
	WOMAN	interactive television, interactive television
	MAN	digital telephony, digital telephony

WOMAN	the Internet, the Internet
MAN	telephone marketing, telephone marketing
WOMAN	mobile radio, mobile radio
MAN	satellite broadcasting, satellite broadcasting

DOING BUSINESS 1   **page 117**
Two views

ALAN DAVIES

When I think of the e-mail technology and its importance to me, I think of it also as being an evolutionary process. When I first started using e-mail back in '86, I really just used it to transmit simple text messages and it took me a while before I understood its potential. Today in '97, I look at that and I think about the phone versus sending messages and for me, the e-mail is a more important technology. And that's not just myself, but I think all of Shell is looking at this technology in this way. This product is not just text, it is digital information, so I can take a sound clip, a video, a graph, a picture, scanned text and convert that into something that can come across the telephone line and sit on my PC. Whereas, with the phone, all that I can do is talk about it.

The other thing that comes into this that's happening now is the mobile office. We have people that are out meeting the customers, yet need to get information from the Shell Centre, and they can dial in from wherever they are in most parts of the world today to get information from the Shell Centre that's up to date, real time and that just wouldn't have been possible without these e-mail packages.

SUSAN FEARN

Well, in my view, e-mail is very definitely a mixed blessing. On the one hand, it enables us to communicate quickly and effectively and to send documents to people. But on the other hand, I think it wastes an awful lot of business time. Probably 75% of the e-mails that I get are not directly relevant. I'm being included in wider circulations and I spend a lot of time every morning looking at e-mails that I really would have been happier not to get at all. I understand that some organisations are establishing e-mail filters, that they're able to programme the computer in such a way that certain key words are picked out and if the e-mail does not contain that key word, for example 'meeting', those e-mails are deleted and that's one way of saving staff time. Other organisations are employing people to sort through the e-mails of their senior executives, so their time is not wasted. So it seems to me, that while saving money and being very cost effective on one level, e-mail is creating an awful lot more hassle on another level.

grammar key

1 Articles

1
1 Ø, the, a	6 the, Ø
2 the	7 Ø, the, the
3 a	8 Ø, the
4 the	9 Ø, the, the
5 an, a	10 a, a, the, Ø

2
1 Ø	7 the	13 the
2 the	8 the	14 Ø
3 the	9 Ø	15 the
4 Ø	10 Ø	16 Ø
5 the	11 Ø	17 Ø
6 Ø	12 the	

2 Comparisons

1
1 highest	5 as high as
2 lowest	6 longer, than
3 lower than	7 the fastest, the slowest
4 higher than	

2
1 It was the most unsuccessful deal I'd ever made.
2 It was the most expensive meal I'd ever paid for.
3 It was the most confusing set of instructions I'd ever read.
4 The chemicals division was the least profitable division (of all).

3
1 The sooner we leave, the earlier we'll arrive.
2 The longer people wait, the more impatient they become.
3 The older I get, the younger I feel!
4 The harder you work, the higher the rewards.

3 Conditionals

1 1 d   2 c   3 e   4 a   5 f   6 b

2
1 If payment is not made by the end of the month, we will be forced to take legal action.
2 Defective items will be exchanged if you produce a receipt.
3 You can learn more about our products if you consult our website http://www.gbpro.co.uk.
4 Your audience won't hear you if you don't speak clearly.

3
1 If I worked in Beijing, I'd learn Chinese.
2 If I took a cut in salary, I'd work fewer hours.
3 If I had more time, I'd take up golf.
4 If I won the national lottery, I'd retire.

4
1 If I had known the post was vacant, I would have applied.
2 If there hadn't been a road accident, I wouldn't have missed my flight.
3 If my mobile phone had been working, I would have got in touch with you.
4 If he had been insured, he wouldn't have had to pay for his medical expenses himself.

4 Countable and uncountable nouns (1)

1
1 a	5 many	8 a heavy
2 a	6 the	9 a few
3 an	7 transports	10 another
4 a		

2
COUNTABLE	UNCOUNTABLE
law	legislation
coin	cash
meal	catering
advert	advertising

3
1 accommodation	3 advice
2 research	4 work

5 Countable and uncountable nouns (2)

1
1 *hair* (not *hairs*)
2 *notice* (not *a notice*)
3 *a pair of scissors* (not *a scissor*)
4 *Paper* (not *A paper*)
5 *good trip* (not *good travel*)
6 *Light* (not *A light*)
7 *of iron and reinforced glass* (not *of an iron and a reinforced glass*)

2
a bottle of perfume	a flash of inspiration
a barrel of oil	a mountain of work
a stroke of luck	a round of applause
a pair of jeans	

3
1 flash of inspiration	5 barrel of oil
2 round of applause	6 mountain of work
3 bottle of perfume	7 stroke of luck
4 pair of jeans	

6 Future forms

1
1 ~~I'm going to give you a lift if you like.~~
2 ~~The agreement will have been expiring by the end of the month.~~
3 ~~She's says she doesn't apply for the vacancy.~~
4 ~~I'll phone you as soon as I will know the price.~~
5 ~~During the course you'll have improved your communication skills.~~

2
On Monday morning he's flying to Berlin. The plane leaves at 16.35 and arrives at 18.05. When he has arrived he'll check into the Regency Hotel.
On Tuesday he's meeting Herr Eicher in the morning and visiting the agent's premises in the afternoon.
On Wednesday morning he's giving a presentation of the first quarter's sales results and in the afternoon he's attending a seminar on 'Selling in Eastern Europe'.
Then on Thursday he'll be driving to Potsdam for a tour of the new offices. Then he's having lunch with Frau Grabe at 1 p.m.

Finally on Friday he leaves Berlin at 10.05 and gets back to
Heathrow at 11.35. He has the afternoon off and will probably
go home and have a well-earned rest.

3
1 will be working   4 will have disappeared
2 will increase   5 will be using
3 will have gone bankrupt   6 will have replaced

7 Linking words

1 1 *b*   2 *c*   3 *a*   4 *c*

2
1 First of all   4 so
2 Secondly   5 In conclusion
3 at the same time

3
1 Although   5 Alternatively
2 nevertheless   6 However
3 As a result   7 On the contrary
4 therefore

8 Must *and* have to

1
1 must/have to   5 don't have to
2 must   6 must/have to
3 must/have to   7 must not
4 must/have to   8 must not

2
a Helmets must be worn.
b You have to give way.
c You must not overtake.
d You must not turn right.
e You have to turn right.
f You must not walk on the grass.
g You must give priority to oncoming traffic.
h You have to pay when parking here between 9.00 and 18.30.

3 1 ~~have to~~   2 ~~have to~~   3 ~~must~~   4 ~~have to~~

9 Nouns in groups

1 1 *a*   2 *c*   3 *a*   4 *b*   5 *a*   6 *a*

2 BOX A: market forces, consumer spending, laser printer,
balance sheet, service industry, chief executive

BOX B: voice mail, brand leader, labour costs, asset stripper,
time limit, ski resort

3
1 management training   4 exchange rate mechanism
   programme   5 quality control procedure
2 world trade centre   6 overseas investment opportunity
3 power generation project   7 needs analysis questionnaire

10 Passive

1 1 *c*   2 *d*   3 *e*   4 *f*   5 *b*   6 *a*

2
1 is recognised   3 has developed
2 has been involved   4 was published

3 *g, f, b, a, d, e, h, c*

11 Past continuous and past perfect simple v. continuous

1 1 *e*   2 *g*   3 *d*   4 *b*   5 *f*   6 *c*   7 *a*

2
1 woke up   14 considered
2 had collapsed   15 believed
3 started   16 decided
4 was   17 thought
5 bought   18 knew
6 sold   19 had entered/was entering
7 thought   20 hit
8 knew   21 plunged
9 was doing   22 had gone
10 became   23 had lost
11 were   24 flew
12 was hiding
13 was not behaving/
    did not behave/
    had not been behaving

12 Past simple and present perfect

1 1 *c*   2 *e*   3 *b*   4 *d*   5 *a*

2
1 Have you ever been   6 Have you ever made
2 went   7 I had to
3 did you stay?   8 did you talk
4 booked   9 presented
5 was

3
1 was   9 (has) got rid of
2 launched   10 has taken
3 sold   11 has set up
4 was   12 has become
5 decided   13 began
6 has been   14 has proved
7 has become   15 was
8 has reorganised   16 made

13 Present perfect simple and present perfect continuous

1
1 have moved   5 have appointed
2 have not changed   6 has been falling
3 have added   7 have increased
4 has moved

2 1 *d*   2 *c*   3 *a*   4 *e*   5 *b*

3
1 have not been   6 have guaranteed
2 have been meaning   7 have been doing/have done
3 have been   8 have not signed
4 have been trying   9 have made
5 have reached

14 Present simple and present continuous

1 Benetton makes clothing.
Yamaha makes motorbikes and musical instruments.
Indesit makes washing machines.
Compaq makes computers.
Nestlé makes chocolate and food products.
Fiat makes motor vehicles.

2
1 Foreign direct investment is growing.
2 Profit margins are soaring.
3 Unemployment levels are declining.
4 Union membership is plummeting.

3
1 are launching   3 costs
2 involves   4 regret

5 is working
6 manufacture(s)
7 owns
8 are perfecting
9 enables, fly
10 am sitting
11 are putting in
12 is trying, looks
13 are organising, require
14 do not understand, depends, mean

15 Quantifiers

1
1 ✔
2 ... a little progress but not much.
3 ... has a different reference number.
4 ... one asks too much.
5 Few expatriates ...
6 Both candidates ...
7 ✔
8 How much time ...
9 There's very little data
10 ✔

2
1 a little
2 few
3 little
4 a little
5 Few
6 a few
7 little
8 a little

16 Relative clauses

1
1 Henry Ford was the man who manufactured the first mass-produced motor car.
2 Alexander Graham Bell was the man who patented the first telephone.
3 Nelson Mandela was the man who became the first black South African president.
4 John Logie Baird was the man who produced the first television pictures.
5 Elias Howe was the man who invented the sewing machine.

2   1 c   2 e   3 b   4 a   5 d

3
1 He works for Quantum, which is an American chemical company specialising in plastics.
2 Sony, which lost the videocassette war in the 1980s, has decided to produce a recordable digital video disc to replace the videocassette.
3 The bank which lent us the money went bust.
4 The branch managers, who worked hard to get it, were all given a pay rise.
5 Imperial Tobacco, whose operating profits are £350 million, is number two in the British cigarette market.
6 They live in a city where the public transport network is excellent.
7 We are making gains in productivity which will make our company even more efficient.
8 She offered to type up the report for me, which was kind of her.

17 Reported statements (1)

1   1 d   2 f   3 c   4 e   5 a   6 b

2
She said that last year total sales amounted to $121m.
She said that we will/would be investing more in R & D.
She said that our market share has/had grown by 18%.
She told us that she doesn't/didn't want to diversify in the immediate future.
She pointed out that net profits this year should be in the region of $300m.
She said that nothing succeeds like success.
She told us that she is/was not planning to increase our debt-equity ratio.

18 Reported statements (2)

1   1 say   2 tell   3 said   4 told   5 told

2
FOLLOWED BY *THAT*	FOLLOWED BY *TO*
point out	offer
feel	promise
insist	tell
say	threaten

3
1 ... to accept 10%.
2 ... seeking legal advice.
3 ... me not to buy shares in BIY.
4 ... to get me a taxi.
5 ... to send me a copy of the feasibility study.
6 ... to withdraw from the project if we deal(t) with their competitors.
7 .... to increase our budget allocation.
8 ... that initial profit projections appear(ed) to be favourable.

19 Reported questions

1
1 They wanted to know where I saw/had seen the advertisement.
2 They asked me why I am/was interested in joining their firm.
3 They wanted to know what attracted me/had attracted me to the post.
4 They asked me how long ago I left/had left ICI.
5 They asked me how well I got on with my colleagues.
6 They asked me if I know/knew how to use EXCEL.
7 They asked me whether I can/could speak English.
8 They wanted to know what other languages I can/could speak.
9 They wanted to know if I have/had the TOEFL or TOEIC.
10 They wanted to know if I have/had any friends living in the USA.
11 They asked me how soon I can/could start.

2
1 Mr Vaughan wanted to know how many items we had to sell before we reach break-even point.
2 Mr Pozetti wanted to know how soon the laboratory samples would be ready.
3 Mrs Cole wanted to know when we last reviewed the complaints procedure.
4 Christine wanted to know whether we should take out political risk insurance for the Albanian consignment.
5 Herr Lüdcke wanted to know how long the guarantee would last.
6 Richard wanted to know which car hire firm we normally used.
7 Elaine wanted to know who was responsible for authorising expenses.
8 Dorothy wanted to know when was the last time we had (had) an order from Patagonia.
9 Mr Gould asked us to check the specifications for order no. 549/Y.

20 Verb + -ing or to- infinitive

1
1 speaking
2 to take over
3 remaining
4 launching
5 to be
6 working
7 to see
8 travelling
9 to provide
10 to buy
11 waiting
12 to appear
13 to refund
14 going out
15 to believe
16 to back
17 moving
18 to improve
19 to give
20 to get

2
1 to purchase
2 to reduce
3 to make
4 paying
5 to hear
6 to receiving

Pearson Education Limited
Edinburgh Gate, Harlow, Essex CM20 2JE England.

© Addison Wesley Longman Limited 1998

Published by Addison Wesley Longman Ltd 1998

Third impression 1999

Set in $10\frac{1}{2}$/13pt Adobe Garamond

Printed in Spain by Graficas Estella

Produced for the publishers by de Henseler Books
Designed by Oxprint Design, Oxford

ISBN 0 582 29879 2

Acknowledgements

With special thanks to Carole Robinson for her input on the pronunciation work.

The publishers and author would like to thank the following people and institutions for their feedback and comments during the development of the material;

Tim Bowen, ILC Hastings; Sally Cassells, Regent Capital Executive Centre; Joy Godwin, Linguarama, Stratford-upon-Avon; Alison Haill, Oxford Professional English Language Training; Howard Thomas, Francis King School; Madeleine du Vivier; Barbara Morris and Nick Barrall, Fontainebleau Langues & Communication; Colleen P. Cheney, Lingua Nova, Warsaw; Nazela Faisali Mahyar; Maggie Hughes.

The author would also like to thank Stephen Nicoll and Kate Goldrick at AWL for their invaluable guidance, and especial thanks to Yvonne de Henseler and Carolyn Parsons for their magnificent support.

We are grateful to Hitachi Home Electronics (Europe) Limited for consenting to the use of the title 'Powerhouse'.

We are grateful to the following for permission to reproduce copyright material:

Nicholas Brealey Publishing Co Ltd for extracts from *THE FRONTIERS OF EXCELLENCE: Learning from Companies that Put People First* by Robert Waterman (1993) and a diagram from *RIDING THE WAVES OF CULTURE* by Fons Trompenaars and Charles Hampden-Turner. New Edition 1997 published by Nicholas Brealey Publishing, 36 John Street, London WC1N 2AT, Tel: (0171) 430 0224, Fax: (0171) 404 8311; The Economist for a short extract from *THE ECONOMIST* 25.12.93-7.1.94 © *The Economist*, London 1994, an adapted extract from the article 'A rescue at sea in South Korea' in *THE ECONOMIST* 26.11.94 © *The Economist*, London 1994, an adapted extract from *THE ECONOMIST* 03.02.96. © *The Economist*, London 1996 and an extract from the article 'Ford 2000' in *THE ECONOMIST* (date unspecified). © *The Economist*, London; Esquire Magazine and the Hearst Corporation for abridged extracts from the article first published as 'Dudes! Get a Life,' by Stanley Bing in *ESQUIRE MAGAZINE*, May 1993; The Financial Times Ltd for adapted extracts from the articles 'Peabody', 'ARC', 'Hanson Brick' in *THE FINANCIAL TIMES* 31.1.96; HarperCollins Publishers on behalf of Fontana for a slightly edited extract *WHAT THEY DON'T TEACH YOU AT THE HARVARD BUSINESS SCHOOL* by Mark McCormack; Haymarket Management Publishing Ltd for slightly adapted extracts from articles 'Time for a smoke break', 'Work hard, fray hard', 'Literally travel-sick blues' in *MANAGEMENT TODAY* June 1996 p12, May 1997 p12. May 1997 p.15; Hodder & Stoughton for an abridged extract from *LIAR'S POKER: Playing the Money Markets* by Michael Lewis. Copyright © 1989 Michael Lewis; Negotiate Ltd and the author, Gavin Kennedy for edited extracts from *EVERYTHING IS NEGOTIABLE* 2nd edition, 1987 (Arrow Business Books Ltd); Newspaper Publishing PLC for an extract from the article 'Man who bets £10bn on a crash ' by Paul Vallely in *THE INDEPENDENT* 19.9.96; Office for National Statistics for text and graph of UK GDP from *SOCIAL TRENDS* 1996–Office for National Statistics. Crown Copyright 1997.

'Coca-Cola' and 'Coke' are registered trademarks which identify the same product of The Coca-Cola Company.

The Publisher would like to thank and acknowledge the following sources for pictures, copyright material and trademarks reproduced on the following pages;

Advertising Archives: 40–41; BBC Archives: 50; Byte: 7 1 & br; Camera Press: 28 tc; Colorific: 85a, 88c; Daewoo: 80; David Evans: 11 tr. 117; Financial Times Picture Library: 16 r, 120; Flamingo: 116; FORD Cars: 52–3; Hulton Getty: 10–11. 103 1; Guardian Picture Library: 60 (Photo: By permission of Roger Bamber); IBM: 114; Johnson & Johnson: 97 b; The Kobal Collection: 4 (Electric Pictures/Columbia Tristar); 9 (Zupnick/Curtis Enterprises); 14 (Zupnick/Curtis Enterprises; 15 (Twentieth Century Fox/Walrus and Associates Ltd); 20 (Twentieth Century Fox/Walrus and Associates Ltd); 26 (Yorktown Productions/Warner Bros Pictures); 30 (Twentieth Century Fox/The American Entertainment Partners); 38–9 (Addis/Wechsler & Associates/Avenue Entertainment); 44 (Alfran Productions); 46–7 (Alfran Productions); 104 (Handmade Films); 106 Twentieth Century Fox/The American Entertainment Partners); 122 Touchstone Pictures/Silverscreen Partners IV); Carolyn Parsons: 111 br; le Petit Blanc Brasserie, Oxford: 111 c; Photographers Library: 103 r; Picador: 99; Pictor Uniphoto: 18–19; 34, 43 tc, cr, & tr, 48, 58, 1, c & r, 90 r, 91 background, 92, 111 tc; Popperfoto: 28 t, 85 e; Rex Features: 24, 28 bc, 56–7, 85 c, d, f & g (in order of descent), 88 tr & br, 97 c, 108 t & b, 110, 121 t; The Rolex Watch Company: 64 1 & r (Photo: P. A. Nicole S.A.); Siemens: 97 t; Tony Stone: 22, 43 bl & cl; Jeff Tabberner: 23 t, 70–71, 75, 90 tl, 96 1: Telegraph Colour Library: 23 b, 31 t & b, 43 tl & br, 76–7, 86, 90 bl, 94 t & b, 102 t, 103 c, 121 b; Topham Picturepoint: 12 l & r, 28 b, 31 (inset), 36 t, 37, 88 1, 91 (inset left and inset centre), 102 b, 115, 118.

Key: t = top   b = bottom   r = right   c = centre   1 = left
For page 85 pictures are listed in order of descent on page.

Cover photograph: © Tony Stone Images (Randy Wells).

Illustrated by: John Martin & Artists, Amanda MacPhail, Edward McLachlan, Oxford Illustrators Oxford, Oxprint Design Oxford